With the
Cape Mounted Rifles

ZULU WARRIOR

With the
Cape Mounted Rifles

Experiences of Kaffir Warfare, Camp Life
and Sport in South Africa

With Illustrations by the Author

Thomas J. Lucas

LEONAUR

With the Cape Mounted Rifles—Experiences of Kaffir Warfare,
Camp Life and Sport in South Africa
by Thomas J. Lucas

Leonaur is an imprint of Oakpast Ltd

Material original to this edition and
presentation of text in this form
copyright © 2010 Oakpast Ltd

ISBN: 978-0-85706-316-8 (hardcover)
ISBN: 978-0-85706-315-1 (softcover)

http://www.leonaur.com

Publisher's Notes

The views expressed in this book are not necessarily
those of the publisher.

Contents

Preface

Though prefaces are somewhat out of date, yet every Author is, I think, justified in saying a few words by way of introduction, were it only for the purpose of supplying the reader with the *raison d'être* of his work.

I may, therefore, I trust, be permitted to observe, that I have endeavoured, in the following pages, to touch upon some of the salient points of life and character in South Africa, and at the same time to weave into them some of the everyday incidents of garrison life—whilst doing duty with my old regiment, the Cape Mounted Rifles, in that country. I have been the more induced to do so from the fact that the. existence of that Corps has now become a matter of history, reasons which are given further on having led to its disbandment.

Some record, therefore, of its constitution and peculiarities may not be out of place in these pages. Its anomalous position as a cavalry regiment, to all intents and purposes, though it was only endowed with infantry rank and pay, marked it out as essentially different from any other corps in Her Majesty's service, whilst its mixed Hottentot and European elements, eminently fitting it for performing with advantage the skirmishing tactics so useful in savage warfare, carried it still further out of the usual category.

With regard to the Cape *ferae,* it has been my wish to

exhibit some of the characteristics of the smaller and more rarely described *fauna,* which, less important as regards size and ferocity, and therefore perhaps less sought after by the sportsman, may yet be found interesting to the general reader, as they certainly will be to the naturalist, whose researches are necessarily more comprehensive.

CHAPTER 1

The Voyage

I will not inflict a detailed account of the sea voyage upon my readers, but simply premise that being appointed to the Cape Mounted Rifle Regiment, serving at the Cape of Good Hope, I took my passage in one of the fine vessels belonging to the General Steam Navigation Company *en route* for that country, touching on the way at the beautiful island of Madeira, where we *did* the convent, purchased the usual amount of feather flowers and *confitures,* duly admired the beautiful Lady Superior, rode one of the little hardy island horses up the almost perpendicular paved roads, which lead to the top of the mountain, and were accompanied by the usual picturesque bandit-looking guide, hanging on to the horse's tail; his hold upon which, much to my disgust, he refused to quit until he had made the ascent. We sighted no more land until we arrived at Ascension, with the exception of a passing view of that very picturesque island off the mainland of the South American coast, St. Fernando de Noronha.

The ordinary crew of the *India* was supplemented by some forty or fifty Lascars, who were shipping back to Calcutta, and who, with their varied and picturesque costumes, made our decks quite gay in the tropical sunlight. It was curious to observe how, in the absence of their own native materials, they had contrived to make gorgeous toilets out of the commonest coloured prints and cotton fabrics; the contrast of colours being always good, and setting off their dusky skins to great advantage—a fact of which they seemed to be perfectly aware. I used to amuse myself by watching them as they prepared their midday meal, the staple dish of which was invariably composed of curry and rice, with the addition of sundry little fish of the sprat genus, known to Indians as *Bombay ducks*, which they picked to pieces-in the most finicking manner with their fingers; about which—to me—there seems always something claw-like. A monkey pulling the husks from a fruit, intently curious to see what it contains, would give-an apt illustration of my meaning. The rice seemed always cooked to a turn, and the whole used to smell most appetising. They were frightfully lazy, and would do nothing without first squatting down on their haunches.

I was told by the first officer, who, much to his disgust, had the supervision of them, that they were-quite unmanageable in bad weather, invariably refusing to go aloft and only encumbering the sailors. In fine weather they worked pretty well, but it generally took two Lascars to do the work of one A. B. Their pay was scanty, and this I suppose made up for it. The most painfully interesting spectacle was to see them on a Sunday morning patiently squatting down on the deck shaving each other. This they did in the most painstaking manner with a blunt razor, without lather of any kind. It made one wince to see hair after hair stubbed up from the roots. Blood-was often drawn during the operation, but it was-endured seemingly as a matter of course, without a murmur.

We had the usual social discomforts on board. First-class passengers looking down on second ditto; who again thought themselves far above the steerage. The *India* was a magnificent ship, built on the lines of a frigate, with a spacious saloon, containing an excellent piano. This would have afforded us a:great deal of rational amusement had it not been always seized upon and monopolised by a bullet-headed German, who played difficult fugues in a distractingly imperfect manner, audibly counting the time to himself the while, and much to the chagrin of a spiteful spinster, who declared that she never could hear a word of the conversation going on around her. As the latter was charmingly interspersed with a great deal of flirtation among the young folks, this was no doubt very distressing. The piano was well clamped down to the deck in case of squalls. Many indeed were the squalls—both maritime and social—to which both it and ourselves were exposed during the voyage. It was certainly a necessary precaution. Imagine, *par exemple*, a lady performer stopping in the midst of an Italian *bravura* to hold on like grim death to the piano (as often happened in rough weather), and painfully oscillating to and fro as the ship rolled from side to side. Who shall say how many quavers there were in the bar in that piece of music! Great was the delight of the spiteful spinster when the German was capsized, stool and all, in the middle of one of his pet fugues, and for once thoroughly discomfited.

I was a mischievous youngster in those days, and cut out a very striking likeness of this old lady on paper; giving proper prominence to the three little corkscrew curls which distinguished her profile. This was maliciously passed round the table at dinner-time, and elicited convulsions of laughter, much to the old lady's surprise, as she never could get to the bottom of the mystery.

So we jogged on, encountering the usual amount of fine and bad weather; "did our storm" in the Bay of Biscay, where we had to hold on to anything that would save us flying overboard, notwithstanding the repeated directions of the captain to "keep her steady;" until we at last sighted that heap of scoria, Ascension. It was, anyway, *terra firma*; and therefore hailed with proportionate delight. We made this island one Sunday, and had the pleasure of seeing the whole available population going to church. It consisted of a detachment of marine artillery, the half dozen storekeepers who supplied the garrison with odds and ends, and the crew of the flagship, which lay at anchor in solitary grandeur. The island is in fact inhabited only as a sanatorium for the navy-squadron employed in watching the slave trade on the west coast of Africa, and possesses a small iron church, a few general stores, and some isolated buildings used as barracks. Such absolute scoria is the soil that no vegetation is to be seen, except that here and there, growing in the chinks of the rock, is found a beautiful pink flower, of the oleander species, flourishing in solitary beauty. So badly is the island supplied with provisions, that the garrison actually draws its principal supplies from its large turtle ponds, supplemented by the eggs of the "wide awake" bird; a species of tern, which deposits its eggs in enormous quantities on the mainland.

This is one of the sights of the island. Imagine an area of some acres of land covered with one compact mass of eggs. Picture to yourself the myriads of birds, packed together during the process of hatching the future brood, and the confused whirring of wings as they pass to and fro, and then you will not wonder that the supply is practically inexhaustible. Children are generally employed to collect the eggs. They first smash indiscriminately all that occupy a sufficient space of ground to ensure a fresh supply on the morrow; and on the next day return and collect them in boxes, each containing some hundreds. These, with a certain portion of turtle flesh, form the rations of the little colony four days out of the seven, and are made to eke out the scanty supply of butcher's meat brought to the island. The eggs are small but well-flavoured and wholesome, and the yolk is of a bright vermilion colour.

The turtle ponds contained, at the time of our visit, some seven hundred and odd magnificent turtles, weighing from one to four hundredweight, and were enclosed in square parks, made of blocks of *tufa*, which admitted the ingress of the tide, and so seemed to keep the inmates in fine condition.

Amongst the passengers was a knowing old major of artillery, who, having made friends during our visit with the naval captain commanding the island, managed to get possession of a fine turtle, which he took with him with the intention of presenting it to his superior officer on his arrival. It was carried the whole way in fine health on the mild refreshment of a bucket of seawater, which was thrown over it twice a day as it lay helplessly on its back like a stranded alderman with a wet swab under its head by way of pillow. As it lay with no power to move itself out of this recumbent position, it looked with its light yellow, unbaked crust-coloured carapace, like a huge raised pie; and one of our amusements was to watch the huge convex surface gradually sinking in (as if the juice had run out) until just before we landed it became perfectly flat.

The day after our arrival at Ascension the *Britomart*, a pretty man-of-war brig, came in. The captain, a gentlemanly, agreeable man, paid the *India* a visit, and soon getting on friendly terms with the passengers, proposed an excursion to the top of the Green Mountain, so called as it contained the only vegetation to be found on the island; for in it was a villa used for a sanatorium for the sick naval officers. The proposition was gladly acceded to, and a trap drawn by two hardy little island horses having been procured for the ladies, the gentlemen started off on foot for a walk some eight miles up the mountain, by a capital winding road cut into the *tufa*. We passed on our way a large covered reservoir of beautiful clear water, which is brought in pipes from the summit, and serves to supply the ships and garrison; and after a pretty stiff climb, we found ourselves in front of a low unpretending building of the villa type, standing in the midst of a really pretty garden filled with roses, fuchsias, balsams, scarlet geraniums, and other homely flowers growing in the greatest luxuriance; whilst bananas and plantains formed a picturesque screen at the back, and fruit trees of various kinds were dotted about on the grass plot.

Here we found two young naval officers, one of whom in the course of conversation accounted for this exceptionally green spot in the following manner.

He said that the seeds of vegetation forming this oasis were supposed to have been dropped by passing birds in the first instance upon the scanty soil made by the detrition of the rocky summit. He added, that as the soil produced by the decomposition of vegetable matter increases, it keeps spreading slowly down the sides of the mountain at the rate of about half an inch in a year, and will, it is supposed, in time materially alter the condition of the island.

These officers seemed rather tired of the monotony of their existence, their only amusements being wild goat and jungle fowl shooting; but stated that the climate is wonderfully temperate and healthy, seldom varying between 60° and 68°. Having exhausted the wonders of the Green Mountain, we made our way back to the *India* after a very pleasant excursion.

On leaving, our captain purchased a turtle about 250 pounds in weight for the vessel, and in consequence, we revelled in turtle soup, cutlets, and steaks, and indeed in turtle in every form for the next fortnight, until we got to understand very easily how it was that the garrison came to complain of their turtle rations, and to sigh for the toughest beef steak in exchange for that delicacy. It led, however, to the production of some excellent rum punch, which was a sufficient consolation.

On nearing St. Helena we fell in with a great number of whales of various kinds. Of the many interesting sights to be met with in a long sea voyage, none could be more striking than an encounter such as we had the good fortune to witness between a whale and his enemy the thresher. We were cruising off St. Helena one morning, when the excited voice of the captain calling through the cuddy skylights brought all the passengers on deck to see a thresher chasing a whale, a sight so unusual, he said, that it had only once come under his observation during the course of his long maritime experience. It was indeed a grand spectacle. No sooner did the whale make his appearance on the surface of the ocean than the thresher, a huge species of shark some thirty feet long, propelled himself suddenly from the water until at least two-thirds of his body were exposed, and apparently whirling his enormous pectoral fins like flails in the air, brought them down, aided by the impetus of his whole weight, with sledgehammer blows upon the unfortunate whale,[1] sending up a shower of spray in a grand column around him as he rose, and striking his victim with such force that the shock was heard on board the steamer almost like the distant boom of a gun; and this at the distance of half a mile. The whale sank

1. This description, records my impression of the *modus operandi* pursued by the thresher in his attacks upon the whale, as seen from the deck of the *India*. Naturalists are, I believe, now of opinion that the thresher inflicts this punishment with the tail, and not with the fins as described. The long flexible nature of his tail seems to favour this hypothesis, though it is difficult to see how it can be brought into play.

rapidly from sight after receiving this punishment, but again rose to the surface after a comparatively short interval, and was no sooner visible than the thresher, who seemed instinctively to divine where he would come up, repeated his attack, followed by the same action. Thus the Homeric battle went on until both whale and thresher were eventually lost in the distance, with what result it was impossible to say.

An old whaling captain who was on board assured me that the whale often succumbs to the persistent assaults of his enemy; and that the circumstance of his rising to the surface so soon after his disappearance is only to be accounted for by the fact (vouched for, as he asserted, by all old whalers) that the thresher is always accompanied on these occasions by a friendly sword-fish, which does its best to stimulate the unfortunate *cetacean* with his sword to come again to the surface, where the confederate awaits him. But whether friendship only or an ultimate share of the spoil is the reward of these services, "this deponent further said not." It was a grand sight, and was hailed at the time with great enthusiasm, as is every incident which tends to break the monotony of a sea voyage; just as the first flying fish and the capture of the first shark is anxiously awaited.

I observed, by-the-bye, a curious parasite, which I have not before seen described, on several flying fish that had flown on board or into the main chains in the dark and were there captured. The tail of this parasite with its black tassel-like appendage, was always found projecting from the sides of the fish; the pink fleshy looking head, with its singular arms projecting on either side of the neck, being buried in the flying fish's body. It measured some two inches in length. Some of the afflicted fish were infested with three or four of these large parasites, which I should think must have made them very uncomfortable. On this voyage we had the opportunity to verify the fact of the dolphin's frequent change of colour before death, showing the most lovely sunset tints, varied with vivid cobalt and gold shades. It is otherwise an ugly round-headed fish, and in no wise remarkable.

Whilst at St. Helena we chartered a fly drawn by two wretched horses, for which we had to pay two guineas, and went the usual round of the island, climbing laboriously up the narrow ledges of roads, *doing* the usual Napoleon sightseeing, and admiring much the beautiful hedges made up of gigantic tree fuchsias and scarlet geraniums, winding up our visit with the worst dinner in the worst inn at the highest possible price it has ever been my lot to encounter.

We left St. Helena and had now reached the zone frequented by the beautiful Cape pigeon, with its butterfly flight and handsomely speckled wings, flitting restlessly and unceasingly in our wake; and many a capture did we make of this pretty bird in a very simple manner, by trailing lengths of white thread from the taffrail. These floating in the air and well nigh invisible, the mere force of the bird's onward career as it struck against them in its flight was sufficient to wrap them round his pinions in a moment, and sometimes to form quite a complicated knot which it was difficult to unravel, and by which the bird was effectually disabled. At times a strong line with a powerful hook baited with a piece of flesh was cast over the stern, being previously fastened to a flat piece of board to keep it afloat on the surface, and a huge soaring albatross, measuring some nine or ten feet from wing to wing, would be triumphantly hauled in. No greater contrast can be conceived than this bird's magnificent appearance as he sweeps the air on his vast pinions, as if "monarch of all he surveys," and his crest-fallen air when brought struggling to the deck. Here all his-grandeur vanishes, and he becomes ludicrously helpless, his waddling gait and awkward movement showing that he is quite out of his element. He is-a most formidable bird notwithstanding, and it is well to keep out of the way of his powerful wings; one stroke of which I am told is sufficient to break a limb.

Beyond the accustomed *votive* offerings to Neptune we had had no sickness of any account on board. This was, all things considered, very fortunate, taking into account the unsatisfactory nature of the medical attendance provided by the company. This was-concentrated in the person of the doctor, a tall angular Scotchman, a most eccentric character, of shy and reserved habits, who passed the greater part of his time leaning over the bulwarks intently regarding the horizon with lacklustre eyes, and talking to himself in a weird and most uncanny manner. He was totally impervious to conversation, and when he did hazard a remark, which was only on rare occasions, mumbled in his speech so dreadfully, and spoke with so strong and full-flavoured an accent, that he was almost unintelligible. He never appeared to occupy himself professionally when he could avoid it, and if wanted on any sudden emergency had to be almost dug out of his berth amidships; so that, at last, only the most unavoidable necessity ever induced any one to apply to him for advice.

So far as his professional capacity was concerned, he was a perfect nonentity, but not so our "culinary doctor" of the "galley," whose indefatigable endeavours to keep seven saucepans going at the same time in his *caboose* of six feet by three, with his entire cuisine oscillating at an angle of forty-five degrees, was a never-failing source of wonder. He always contrived, in the heaviest weather, to turn out a capital dinner, soup included, when, in spite of fiddles and other nautical contrivances, the joints positively took wing, and potatoes rolled out of tureens to and fro upon the long dining tables in lively procession, and were skilfully harpooned in passing, and the carver had to hold on by his eyelids. Should illness intervene, was there not the captain's medicine chest with its inexhaustible supply of remedies to look to? But where eating and drinking formed the main object of existence, what should we have done without our "doctor *par excellence*"—the cook?

I must not forget to mention amongst the most inveterate victims to *mal de mer* an old Roman Catholic priest, one Father Watkins, a Welshman, who in ordinary times was the life of the saloon. He had been doing duty in the interior of the Cape for more than thirty years, amidst every difficulty, and had by his own exertions raised subscriptions for building a church in the desolate part of the country where he had made his abode. He was a regular *bon garçon* and had, he said, a dispensation from the Pope to fast when he thought proper; which penitence was only exercised when minute enquiry had convinced him that the dinner was to be worse than usual. He was our best whist player,

17

and was always to the fore when any fun was going on, his ruddy face beaming with satisfaction and his little twinkling grey eyes brimming over with jollity. Unfortunately, he never could make friends with Neptune in bad weather, but lay, a warning to all free livers, completely prostrate in his berth, very much like a porpoise which had stranded helplessly in shallow water. He was a kind-hearted old man,—"may his shadow never grow less."

On fine evenings we were not unprovided with music for the mazy dance, an orchestra having been improvised by three soldiers of the line who were drafted to St. Helena, one of whom, an old bandsman, had shown his musical proclivities by converting an old flour-barrel into a very respectable drum by covering the top with the skin of one of our slaughtered sheep. This with the addition of a clarionet, a tambourine, and a pair of cymbals operated upon by the drummer's little boy, was quite sufficient to set many willing pairs of feet going. The longest voyage, however, cannot last forever, and we soon had the pleasure of sighting the imposing headland, Table Mountain, with pretty Cape Town spreading at the base, its white buildings glistening in the sun, and dotted here and there with the greenest of foliage; and the lovely bay filled with innumerable sailing boats flitting to and fro, busily employed in unloading the numerous craft in the offing, whilst whale boats plying about full of Malays in their picturesque costumes crowned by their enormous reed hats, lent life and colour to the scene.

CHAPTER 2

Cape Town

To the tired traveller after his monotonous voyage, which is at best but a pleasant captivity, or as Dr. Johnson puts it, *"imprisonment with the chance of getting drowned,"* Cape Town is charmingly pretty, framed in as it is by the ever picturesque Table Mountain, and enshrined in rich foliage. The stately fir, the home-looking oak, of which there is an abundance, are interspersed with the charming *protea (Protea argentea)* or silver tree of the colonists, with its magnolia-like flowers distilling honey from its beautiful cup-like blossoms, and softening the landscape by the subdued hue of its silvery leaves. I will not add to the already voluminous descriptions of the town itself. Its fine parade (the Heerengracht) with its *umbrageous* pine-trees, and the excellence of its *tables d'hôte* are well-known. Mrs. Parkes still keeps up her ancient "prestige" as a caterer of the *premiere classe,* and her hospitable mansion was at the time of which I treat, principally supported by the numerous Indian officers and civilians who made this healthy settlement their universal retreat.

These were the palmy days of Cape Town, as the Indians not only contributed largely by their lavish expenditure and luxurious requirements, to the resources of the settlers; but in numerous instances found mates and carried off many of the Cape *belles,* who have always been remarkable for personal attractions.

Society is notably very agreeable in this hospitable part of the world, where visitors are universally welcomed and entertained, and balls, dances, "reunions," of all kinds are almost necessaries of existence amongst these pleasure-loving people.

Alas, in one respect, *nous avons change tout cela,* Indian officers and civilians were privileged in those days to spend their terms of leave at the Cape, at the same time retaining their full-pay and allowances; but if they went to England were relegated to half-pay forthwith. Consequently they naturally preferred recruiting their shattered frames in this temperate latitude, and enjoying its hospitalities, to going further and faring worse, in many respects; not the least drawback being the uncongenial nature of the home climate after the burning heats of the East—the Cape being thus, in more senses than one, literally halfway between the two extremes. Since, therefore, the new regulations have placed the Cape on the same footing with regard to allowances, and there is now no pecuniary advantage to be enjoyed, it is not surprising that Indians should prefer to extend their route to England, whither so many home associations attract them. But it can well be imagined how these golden times are looked back upon with anxious yearnings by the community of Cape Town, more especially on the part of the marriageable young ladies, who have lost their opportunity of securing those eligible *partis.*

One of my pleasantest recollections of Cape Town is connected with a visit that I paid to my friend Major A., whose acquaintance I had previously made on the frontier. He was an old and distinguished officer in the Indian Horse Artillery, well-known not only for his wit and *bonhomie,* but as a highly educated scientific man, whose contributions to the military journals had gained him a high reputation in India. He was, moreover, remarkable in other ways. He was one of the three prisoners taken captive by the Chinese in their first war with England, and was, with Captain and Mrs. Douglas, his companions in captivity, carried up the country. They were cooped up in bamboo cages, and, after a prolonged durance, only restored to liberty at the conclusion of the hostilities, when Mr.

Commissioner Lin was induced to exchange them as prisoners of war with some of our Chinese captives.

The Major was an enormous man, a good six feet high, and weighing some twenty stone, with a huge red beard, a deep rich voice, and a sagacious massive face, brimming over with jollity. He had a habit, when not otherwise employed, of pacing restlessly backward and forward to the full extent of his long saloons, which were connected by folding-doors, and having at either end a table with a bottle of sherry on one and a bottle of port on the other. Imagine this enormous man in a perpetual state of perspiration (the weather being very hot) with his coat off, and continually mopping himself with a large napkin, like a young tablecloth, which he carried tucked up under his arm, perpetually plying, as it were, between the two rooms, fortifying himself at starting with a glass of sherry at No. 1 table, varied by a glass of port at No. 2 when he reached the other end, and puffing away, in the meanwhile, at an immense cheroot, which never seemed to go out, so constantly was it replaced, and rolling forth one continuous stream of anecdote, fun, and wisdom, and some idea can be formed of the Major's peculiarities. Such a conglomeration of constant stimulant, tobacco-smoke, and intellectual activity I never met with. As a companion he was simply delightful.

He was an enthusiastic soldier, and had travelled some hundreds of miles up the frontier for the purpose of making himself acquainted with the ins and outs of Kaffir warfare. Nothing could be imagined more incongruous than the presence of this stout warrior, habited in his free-and-easy civilian attire, totally unarmed, puffing away at the inevitable cheroot, with a binocular slung over his ample shoulders, "larding the lean earth" as he moved about on foot, whilst we were skirmishing in the bush, and taking everything as coolly as if he were enjoying his usual morning promenade. As we sat round the bivouac fire who so jolly and full of fun as he! After his return from the campaign he had taken a pretty cottage ornée, which he termed his bungalow, at the charming village of Wynberg, a few miles from Cape Town. Here he was waited upon by his Indian servant Hyder, who was a superb cook, and astonished us at times with the most recondite dishes. Nothing seemed too difficult for his culinary powers, and I remember his surprising us one day by producing an excellent imitation of Devonshire cream, which he served up in glasses, and which was most delicious. How he managed it I do not know. Poor Hyder! He had enough to do during the day to answer the frequent demands of his master, who was always ringing the little hand-bell in the saloon, and calling out for *brandy-pawnee*, to which stimulant he applied himself as a sort of interlude between the pauses of No. 1 and 2 tables. This wonderful mixture of liquors seemed to have no effect whatever upon his seasoned frame, except perhaps to draw out his conversational powers and to make him, if possible, more genial.

His adventures in China alone supplied him with an inexhaustible fund of anecdote. He was, he told me, out surveying at some distance from a fort in the suburb of some Chinese town, and leisurely carrying on his work, when the sudden appearance of a crowd of Chinese from a neighbouring village warned him of his danger. He was soon overpowered by numbers, and suddenly felled to the ground by a blow from some missile, when they swarmed in upon him, and one of them began battering his knees with a large stone, by way of rendering him more helpless. In this unpleasant position he had the presence of mind to sham insensibility, and described how, through his half closed eyelids, he could plainly perceive one of the yellow ruffians pertinaciously tugging away at a valuable ring on his finger, and at the same time feeling behind him with the other hand for his knife, with the evident intention of cutting off the finger for the purpose of securing it. This, he said, was rather a thrilling moment; the ring, however, luckily yielded in time to prevent this undesirable result.

After placing him in a bamboo cage, which was so small that it did not admit of his even sitting upright, he was carried off on poles like a package of tea on the shoulders of the Chinese bearers from village to village; receiving at his halting-places all kinds of delicate attentions in the shape of showers of dead cats, rotten eggs, to say nothing of a choice-repertory of abuse and foul language, and was finally lodged in the courtyard of a temple or joss-house, in the interior, where he turned his artistical talent (for he was a most accomplished artist) to account by painting portraits of the mandarins who thronged to see the "great red barbarian" as they called him. The remuneration was so many mutton pies per portrait; there being a mutton, or more probably I suppose, a bow-wow-pieman, established with his-stand near the place of his captivity, which, as he was not too well fed having regard to his physique and gustatory powers, he resorted to as a means of improving his bill of fare. Here he seems to have played all sorts of practical jokes upon his visitors. Being let out upon parole after a time (as there was no chance of his escape) he related how he seized the opportunity one day when his tormenters were absent to make his way into the *penetralia* of the temple, and climbing the shrine where reposed the hideous-little Chinese god, the form of which is so familiar to us in curiosity collections, to abstract the same and leave in its place a wooden match box from the best German factories (one of our own household gods). He described his delight, when the ensuing day brought the usual crowd of admiring devotees to prostrate themselves before the shrine, little dreaming of the metamorphosis which their deity had undergone under the auspices of the "great red barbarian."

I am digressing, however, lamentably from my narrative. Wynberg itself is as delightful a country village as can well be imagined. It is intensely Dutch, in its trim houses with their green shutters-and formal avenues, the latter backed up by the grand Table Mountain with its beautiful *protca* plantations; at the same time it is quite tropical, being adorned on all sides with beautiful heaths, fuchsias, aloes, prickly pears, Hottentot figs, and other eastern types of vegetation, and revels in a delicious climate tempered by its proximity to the sea, whilst quite sheltered from, the violent south-east wind so prevalent in Cape Town—the latter indeed forming the great drawback to this otherwise pleasant city.

When the south-east wind is strong, the summit of Table Mountain, which is quite flat, becomes shrouded in dense mist that takes the form of a solid cloud of dazzling white vapour hanging over the summit. This peculiarity called "the laying of the table cloth" has a very beautiful effect. The south-east wind blows with such fury that it is almost impossible to make head against it, the loose red sandy soil being whirled about in perfect columns, and the unfortunate pedestrian is positively pelted with all sorts of debris, from grit to actual pebbles. The red dust is so fine that it penetrates everywhere in a most extraordinary manner, even forcing its way through the closed doors and windows, and powdering everything plentifully.

This may well be called the Cape of Storms. I remember a very striking proof of the aptness of this memorable title. The harbour contains at all times a vast fleet of fishing-boats of from one to five tons burden which are moored to buoys at night in close proximity to the shore. Soon after my arrival, I was one morning after a sou' easter looking out of my bedroom window which faced the bay, and wondering what had become of the fleet of fishing-boats not one of which was visible, when my attention was directed to the appearance of innumerable points projecting from the surface of the water surrounding the harbour. Minuter inspection proved these to be nothing more or less than the tops of the masts of the fleet of fishing-boats, which were all submerged, having gone down bodily at their moorings, their short mooring-chains preventing their rising with the swell of the enormous waves, and effectually swamping them one after the other. Later on in the day, the fishermen were to be seen busily employed fishing their boats up again to the surface. This, I am told, is quite an every-day occurrence, nor did the fleet seem any the worse for the accident.

Nowhere can grander seas be met with than here. Whilst standing on the shore, I have repeatedly observed large one-thousand-ton ships completely lost to sight as to their hulls in the troughs of the huge waves which reared their stupendous masses in the bay. At intervals along the coast might be seen the wrecked hulls of stranded ships-which had gone ashore on this ominous coast. Table-Bay has long borne a famous, or rather infamous reputation for its many cases of wilful wreckage; unseaworthy craft being often heavily insured, and brought out here purposely to be lost, being cut 'from their moorings at night and quickly abandoned by their crews to drift on shore in the darkness. Many vessels are on the other hand compelled unavoidably to cut their cables in bad weather (the holding ground being very bad, and the amount of money claimed in consequence by the Malay sailors and fishermen for salvage of anchors is sometimes very great. These Malay fishermen form a very picturesque element of the population of Cape Town, with their pleasing features and singular conical reed hats, which appear to me to be most out of place and unfitted for sailors exposed to the violent Cape hurricanes. I never could understand how they were kept on the heads of the Malay boatmen, a single chin-strap being the only security.

The lighters for unloading the vessels which lie some miles out in the offing, are boats of two or three tons, carrying big sails, and will stand a good deal of sea and surf; but the boatmen cannot be induced to leave the shore when it is blowing hard, so dangerous is the sea, and as gales are of constant occurrence, ships are often detained for long periods in the offing. "Lightering" for passengers is often very expensive, as the boatmen in such times can make their own terms, and will not undertake the risk without corresponding advantage. I have known as much as two guineas demanded in stormy weather for landing a passenger, the ordinary fare being about three shillings. The harbour presents altogether a bustling scene, with its numerous craft, swarms of divers and ducks of various kinds streaming restlessly to and fro, and sometimes quite darkening the air.

The Malays are a steady, thriving people, vastly superior in every way to the Fingoes or Hottentots, and are always cleanly and well clothed. Their religion forbids them to drink, and they have a genius for saving; many of them being established in large businesses, and responsible employment. They are capital drivers, and are to be seen daily "tooling" their four-in-hand omnibuses and country carts, plying between Wynberg, Rondebusch, and the adjoining suburbs, handling the ribbons in a most workmanlike style. They are good servants and famous cooks; but unfortunately have their furious as well as their lucid intervals. During the periodical Mohammedan festivals they excite themselves with narcotics,. under the influence of which they will gash themselves with knives, and go through the most diabolical ceremonies, ending sometimes by "running a muck," and stabbing, with their long Malay *krisses*, any unfortunates who come in their way, inflicting terrible wounds before they can be secured. At ordinary times, however, they are extremely peaceable, well-behaved citizens.

The harbour abounds in fish, amongst which "Stump-nose," "Seventy-four," "Roman-nose," and other strangely named but well flavoured fish are-pre-eminent. Perhaps the most numerous of the finny tribe is the *snook*, a coarse fish resembling our hake, excepting that it has brilliant orange markings about the head. It is taken with hook and line literally by thousands. This is equally with the hake the poor man's fish, and is sold very cheap; and when salted down forms a very important item of the people's food. Cray-fish are very plentiful, and are indeed sometimes found lying about on the beach but are too leathery and substantial to my fancy. New Zealand is the only place where I have ever tasted them really good. There, strange to say, from what cause I know not, they are as succulent, tender,. and well-flavoured as the best lobster.

I had the good fortune during my stay here, to witness a whale chase, though too far out, unhappily, for minute observation. I could see the boats towed along out to sea at a fearful rate, and observed the wounded whale coming up every now and then to spout, and could quite imagine the excitement it must afford to those actually engaged in it. I watched them until almost out of sight with rapt attention. I heard afterwards that the whale eventually escaped. From the universal prevalency of whale-boats, which are now used to land passengers in the bay, Cape Town must have been at one time a great whaling station. These chases are now, I believe, of comparatively rare occurrence, the whale having almost deserted these busy shores. Their bones and *debris,* however, are met with, lying about in all directions.

The observatory at the Cape is "world renowned," and is presided over by a very clever astronomer, a Mr. Maclure. The clearness of the atmosphere, and consequent brilliancy of the constellations being most remarkable. The Southern Cross shows here in all its splendour. The Botanical Gardens, which are very extensive, contained amongst other curiosities two veteran African tortoises, which, according to competent authorities, had attained the respectable age of some two hundred and odd years, and were still youthful and lively in their movements.

Whilst quartered at the Castle barracks, I had the pleasure of making the acquaintance of Dr. Collis Browne, now well-known as the inventor of chlorodyne, that universal soother of miseries, a valuable medicine, which has indeed won him a European reputation. He was a staff-doctor, unattached, at the time I knew him, and I am the more induced to recall our near neighbourhood, as it was in his rooms that I first made the acquaintance of the *ferae naturae,* so well represented in the colony.

It happened in this way. I was in the habit of going to his rooms to have a chat, *sans ceremonie,* as is usually the case in barracks. Dropping in one morning, I was talking to Mrs. Browne, who was seated at a table writing, when, suddenly rising from her chair, she uttered a shriek and rushed into her bedroom, where she shut herself in. I looked on in amazement, but presently discovered the cause of her terror—for a singular undulating movement under the carpet disclosed the presence of a large snake. I called out to the doctor, who was in the next room, to warn him of the advent of his ill-timed visitor; and, we arming ourselves with the first weapons that came to hand—*viz.,* the poker and shovel—routed the "vermin" out of its hiding-place, and *chivied* it under a chest of drawers, where it was despatched, and proved to be a fine specimen of yellow cobra, five feet long. Our quarters were at the top of a flight of stairs on the first-floor; and I can only account for its appearance on the supposition that it had climbed up through the outer wall, which was very massive, but hollow in the centre. It probably had its hole somewhere at the base.

Dr. Collis Browne was a curious instance of a self-made inventor. He was a very clever fellow, but did not find his profession sufficiently remunerative, and so suddenly took it into his head to study how he could set about the invention of something (no matter what) which should supply some general want, and thus commend itself to the public and of course turn ultimately to that consummation so desirable to be attained—his own advantage. I remember that he first tried his "'prentice hand" at a species of water-proof under vest or chest-protector, which was made hollow and intended to be inflated with air, and which he presumed would interpose an effectual barrier against the influx of the cold outer air in cases of weak chest or pulmonary debility. To my astonishment, on looking into his room one morning, I found him in his shirt-sleeves, busily employed cutting out strips of mackintosh with a huge pair of scissors, and gluing them together with some preparation which he was heating over the fire in a pipkin, the whole room being strewn with his materials, and the furniture in a general state of stickiness; his wife looking on, laughing at his eccentricities.

This first essay was, as far as I remember, a failure. He went on I know to many other ventures before he hit upon his grand discovery of chlorodyne, which ought to have made his fortune. Whether it turned out to be of any substantial benefit I do not know! I am afraid that inventors being as a rule poor men, are unable to find the funds to push forward their schemes, and are often obliged to resort to some moneyed speculator, who perhaps makes his fortune upon the fruits of their talents, and takes the lion's share of the profits. I hope this was not his case.

When I first made his acquaintance he was just recovering from a dangerous low fever, which had so prostrated him that he was reduced to a mere skeleton, and for some time, whenever he attempted to walk, his knee-joints used to crack in a most horrible manner. He took to himself all the credit of his own cure, and I am afraid made himself rather unpopular with the medical authorities, to whom, as his military seniors, he had to submit. This was always done against the grain, as he declared that the longer they were in the service, the less they knew. He gave them the credit of a little antiquated knowledge at start-

28

ing, but declared that as they seldom kept up their professional studies after entering the service, the progress of modern science soon left them hopelessly in the rear, and their practice he characterised in many instances as barbarous and obsolete. With such sentiments he was, as may be imagined, often in hot water with his seniors, and he sometimes positively chafed at being obliged to carry out their antiquated treatment of hospital cases. I fancy he did not remain long in the service, and I dare say his superiors were as glad to be rid of him as he to quit, and that there was little love lost between them.

Cape Town possesses a fine library, to which visitors have free access, and the buildings as a rule are spacious and imposing. The fashionable quarter of the town is at Green Point, which is situated at the eastern extremity of the bay, the road to it being the fashionable drive frequented by the Cape aristocracy, and is studded with charming villas standing in pretty gardens. There is abundance of fine fruit in the markets, oranges, bananas, loquots, peaches. watermelons, and grapes being plentiful. Especially worthy of note are the nectarines. Some of which I partook at the *table d'hôte* were as large as one's fist and at the same time well flavoured. The muscatel and sweet-water grapes and a fine fleshy well-flavoured variety called *hanne poot*, or more commonly, "honey pot," are all especially good, though not always in a wine making point of view. The latter, for instance, though delicious to the taste, is said to be too mucilaginous to make good wine.

Everyone, as a matter of course, makes the usual pilgrimage to the two Constantias, Little and Great, to taste the luxurious liqueur wine of that name. To my taste it is too cloying. Strange to say, the ordinary white wine, or Cape sherry, has, from some quality in the grape, an unpleasant earthy taste and odour, and is thin and acid, being seldom drunk by the better class of colonists. There is also Pontac, sweet and dry, a thick syrupy wine between Tent and elderberry, which is dignified in England by the name of African Port, but is only fit to be drunk mixed with water as a refresher. In the way of spirit, there is Cape smoke, a coarse kind of peach brandy with something of the character of gin, with a raisiny flavour, a very rank spirit, though I have known it much liked when the first disagreeable impression has worn off. It is nectar, however, to the Hottentots, who drink themselves insensible upon it when they can get the chance; in which case they lie about the roads, highways, and byways, often in the most exposed places, so that it is difficult to avoid driving over them, as they remain just where they have fallen until time has restored their scattered senses. The hotels are cheap enough considering their excellent accommodation, the charge for *pension* seldom exceeding 7s. 6d. *per diem*.

I did not make a prolonged stay at Cape Town, but took my passage by a small sailing vessel to Algoa Bay (Port Elizabeth), where we landed in a whale boat, both lady and gentlemen passengers being carried on shore by huge Fingoes, whose only clothing was a short linen skirt rolled up above their waists, crowned here and there by an old military *shako*.

CHAPTER 3

Port Elizabeth

Port Elizabeth is a barren, desolate-looking place. The town lies scattered along the inhospitable shore, upon which beats ceaselessly and sullenly the heavy dangerous surf, which takes the shape of long rollers that, breaking eventually in heavy masses upon the beach, make the landing a matter of considerable danger. The universal whale boat must be kept with its bows mathematically straight to the waves, to ensure safety; as the slightest twist broadsidewards. leads to inevitable swamping. The scantily-clad Fingoes have a hard time of it, landing passengers and cargoes, but take it all very good temperedly. The irregularly built town is shut in by steep hills almost bare of vegetation, where stand the better class of houses belonging to the merchants. There is nothing picturesque about the place. Here, however, we found a very comfortable hotel with a liberal table, and but for the unwelcome presence of swarms of rats, a most desirable halting-place.

The rats had an uncomfortable habit of running over my legs when in bed, and made so much racket in their gambols, that I awoke several times under the impression that someone was busily employed removing the furniture, and dragging it about. It did not prevent my sleeping, as I am an old traveller, and familiarity, in my case, has contributed to breed a certain amount of contempt for such trifling *désagréments*. But I can imagine that such an interruption to slumber at night might be very disagreeable to a more sensitive tourist. I have entered my room in the middle of the day and discovered the rats sitting comfortably on the window-sill, looking with a curious eye at my personal effects, and at last discerned how it was that they came to honour my particular *diggins* so frequently with their presence. I found out that it was situated directly over the stables in the court-yard, where, no doubt, a large colony was established, and as the weather was very sultry, my windows were always left wide open, *et voilà tout*. It certainly suggests the propriety of inspecting one's surroundings before fixing one's *locale,* especially in a ratty neighbourhood.

On my return from New Zealand some years since the great 1100 ton ship in which my wife and self had taken our passage literally swarmed with these vermin. Just outside our cabin door hung a quantity of wooden cages containing a whole colony of foreign birds—Java sparrows, spice birds, and every variety of songster and chirper. These innocent little passengers were besieged by hordes of rats, which clung by their claws to the cages frightening the poor little dickeys out of their wits. The fluttering of this host of little wings sometimes kept us awake for hours; and "many a time and oft" have I got out of bed to make a raid upon the rats and effect a temporary diversion on behalf of their victims.

My wife, who stands in much awe of these loathsome animals, always retired to rest with a strong impression of rats upon her mind; and one night I was surprised at being awakened suddenly with the exclamation, "Oh, there's a rat in the bed." I tried to pooh-pooh the matter, but could not argue her out of the impression for some time. She was convinced at last, and once more subsided into the land of dreams. I was dozing off myself, when I suddenly became aware of the passage over the pillow between our two heads of something with a long tail, which disappeared behind the head of the berth; and there on the pillow was plainly to be traced the filthy smear left by the rat in his passage over the white linen surface. I kept my discov-

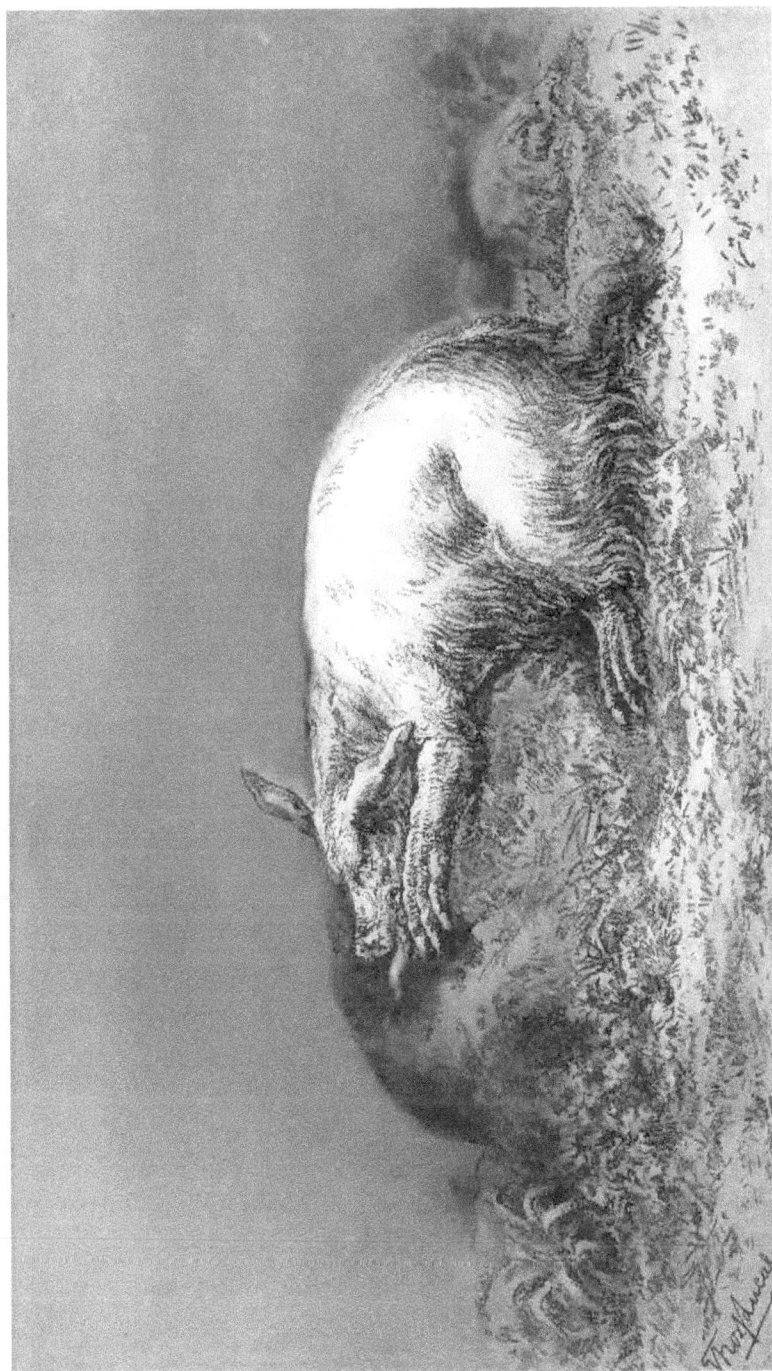

ANT-BEAR FEEDING

ery to myself, and, thinking I had seen the last of our nocturnal visitor, dropped off into a doze. Presently I awoke with a start; something was running over my knees, under the clothes this time, and I remembered the rat. My sudden start had unfortunately aroused my wife, who exclaimed, "Oh, I am sure that was the rat that frightened you." I still tried to convince her to the contrary, and to make light of it, but finding that she was fast verging into the regions of the *hysterical*, I conceded that perhaps it was a mouse, and that if she would jump out and take refuge on a neighbouring box and wrap herself up well, I would try to unearth it.

This she did; when I carefully took layer after layer of clothing off the bed, and when I got to the sheet found my friend an enormous blue rat careering gaily round the berth. I said nothing, but quietly getting hold of a Turkish towel which hung suspended over one of the beams, popped it over him, and inserting my right hand underneath, gripped his throat between my finger and thumb. When my wife heard his dying squeaks she exclaimed, "Oh, I know it's a rat," but as she could not see over the berth, I convinced her it was a mouse, and she passed the rest of the night in tranquillity. When, however, on the next morning, she caught sight of the defunct rat in a pail of water, into which I had quietly dropped it, she was horrified at finding that it was not a mouse after all.

At Port Elizabeth I was fortunate enough to fall in with an officer of the Rifle Brigade who was bound, like myself, to the frontier headquarters at Graham's Town, some 260 miles distant. We accomplished the journey on horseback, chartering for our baggage an ox wagon, which served for house and home and made us quite independent.

The Cape ox-wagon is quite an institution, and has been called, like the camel, the "ship of the plains." The body of the vehicle, some fifteen or sixteen feet in length, is very strong, being made of tough wood put together very loosely, so as to accommodate itself to the frightful jolting it encounters on the African roads. It is not so cumbrous as our English wagons, or so strongly built, the wheels are smaller and the spokes slighter.

It is covered with a strong canvas tent or *tilt* stretched upon a framework of bamboo, and is worth, when new, from sixty to sixty-five pounds. The oxen are *reimed* together by the horns, and are *inspanned* in couples by means of a yoke of heavy wood, which rests horizontally upon their necks. The *trock tow* or main rope by which the wagon is drawn is made of twisted hide fastened to the yoke. The oxen are not guided by reins as in the mule wagons, but are led in difficult places by a *foer louper*, or runner, generally a Fingo or Hottentot boy, who guides the leading oxen with a short rein of untanned leather, and checks their pace or stops them when required by pelting them with a shower of dirt or small stones. Besides the *foer louper* there is a driver who sits in front of the wagon, and when necessary administers the most tremendous punishment to the oxen with a long tapering lash, which he whirls about him very dexterously, and then brings down with an astounding smack, like the report of a pistol, that may be heard on a quiet day for miles. In the hands of a brutal driver it is a terrible instrument of torture; the unfortunate oxen being sometimes completely scored by its merciless thong. There is generally a third performer sitting also in front of the wagon, whose business it is to punish the wheelers with an after *sjambok*, or thick strip of sea-cowhide; the driver's time being generally taken up in running along beside the wagon to get more purchase for the exercise of his long unwieldy whip. This is the accepted mode of travelling, where heavy baggage is concerned, and besides carrying some two or three tons dead weight, the vehicle is filled up with stretchers and bedding, provisions, and everything required for a long journey in the colony, or over the sea-like flats in the interior. When heavily laden, the bedding is placed on the ground at night under the wagon, which forms an *extempore* four-poster for the tired traveller, who is sure at all events of fresh air; and we found it a most enjoyable plan in sultry weather.

We passed through a fine undulating country, fringed here and there with dense bush of mimosa, and all kinds of thorny scrub. Of all these the *vacht een bietjie*, or "wait a bit," is the most formidable, being furnished with sharp curved thorns pointing different ways alternately. Well does it deserve its title; once entangled in its meshes the only means of release is by tearing through, for the thorns are like so many fish hooks, and you come out from the encounter with your clothing torn to shreds.

I noticed a variety of beautiful creeping plants; amongst others a small species of climbing aloe hanging suspended from the bushes bordering the roadside. Several kinds of jessamine loaded the air with perfume, and we were constantly riding over rare bulbs; the ground covered in places with a perfect carpet of large pink convolvulus and Cape violets. Bordering the streams we found fine specimens of the Belladonna-lily growing luxuriantly. Lovely heaths adorn the plains, attaining a height of ten or twelve feet, burdened with blossom. Anon, our road led through some rocky pass, or *kloof,* from whose summit came the harsh grunts of the enormous baboons which regarded us with evident curiosity, the flight of the startled *duyker* and *griesbok* lending interest to the landscape, and whose rocky sides echoed almost musically to the resounding crack of the whip.

At night the oxen were *outspanned* and allowed to scatter whither they would in search of grass, often straying for miles into the bush, to be recalled next morning by a volley of cracks from the long whip, which never failed to bring them straggling in from all directions. The *inspanning* was only to be accomplished with a display of hard swearing and a deal of perspiration. The large-horned oxen adjured by their various names, *En-glaand*, *Blau bok* (blue buck), *Roe cop* (red head), or whatever they might be, to come and submit themselves to the yoke. The demand commencing in a coaxing undertone, and invariably ending in an angry shriek as the perverse beast refused to be brought into position.

My travelling companion I found on acquaintance to be a careless, good-tempered, harum-scarum youngster. He had, with an utter disregard of expense, provided himself with a most extravagant outfit, and appeared to buy everything by the half-dozen. His wardrobe seemed to contain everything that was unnecessary and was mostly ill-adapted to a country like the Cape, including, amongst other items, two cover hats of a bright scarlet colour. He had exhibited to me at various times five or six rifles, with guns of various calibres, to say nothing of pistols, and he had two complete cases of bows and arrows of the most approved archery pattern, and a quantity of knives of all sizes, from the American Bowie down to the murderous little weapon made expressly to be carried in an almost invisible slit of a pocket in his pantaloons; whilst to sum up, he was provided with two Australian stock-whips and a *boomerang*.

The stock-whip, which has a short handle and a solid tapering lash some three yards long, when perfectly handled (which requires a great deal of practice), cracks like the report of a gun, and from the great length of its lash, requires a clear space of some yards for its exercise. Consequently, when my friend, who was a beginner, took it in hand (which was one of his favourite amusements on the halt), he generally commenced his futile efforts without a word of warning, and the company in general had to keep a good look out that it didn't end in their having an eye flicked out by its erratic movements. The *boomerang*, too, was a constant source of terror to both of us; as, though he managed to throw it into the air with great force and dexterity, we could never calculate with any certainty the precise direction which it might take on its return. It oscillated about in the most erratic manner, and generally wound up by hitting one of us a violent crack on the head before it could be caught by the handle, the latter a trick only to be acquired by constant use. As it was made of the hardest iron wood, and had a cutting edge like a knife on its concave surface, this was no joke, though it seemed to afford a good deal of amusement to my erratic friend.

On our arrival at Graham's Town I joined my regiment, and felt myself at once at home amongst my brother officers, whom I found to be a very pleasant gentlemanly set, and I look back to this period as one of the happiest in my life.

CHAPTER 4

Graham's Town

Graham's Town is built in a valley surrounded by rocky hills, and is very badly placed, being ill-supplied with water; the little half-dry stream that runs-through it (which is, I believe, a branch of the river Cowie) having little claim to the latter appellation. The town consists principally of one long street of straggling irregular houses, with a broad road between planted with dwarf trees. There are no buildings worthy of note, except the handsome stone prison, which stands on an elevated position overlooking the town. The *drostdy* barracks, which contain the Government House, is a long unpretentious building. Some well-built quarters, principally apportioned to artillery and engineer officers, are alone worthy of the name. The infantry barracks at Fort England, and the cavalry barracks, with the exception of their respective mess-houses, which are good stone buildings, are of a wretched, unsubstantial character.

The Cape Mounted Rifle Regiment was some 800 strong, and consisted of twelve troops, two-thirds of whom were composed of Europeans recruited from other regiments; the remainder being Hottentots. They were well mounted and a very serviceable corps, well adapted for the work for which they were intended, *viz.*, skirmishing and patrolling through the large tracts of country which we included in our frontier possessions. The

Hottentots were specially fitted for this duty, having a wonderful eye for country, and being noted for their cleverness in tracing the faintest *spoor* or track left upon the *veldt* by man or beast. This they were sometimes called upon to do even in time of peace, although there was a Kaffir police organized for this and other purposes connected with the native administration. They were seldom at fault, generally returning with the missing oxen, which they sometimes traced far into the interior. They were very fair shots, having a natural aptitude for anything requiring quickness of hand and eye, and would mount their horses bare-backed at a moment's notice, using their halters as bridles, and dashing off at full speed to recapture stray horses, when on patrol or camp duty. They wore a rifle uniform, with the addition of cavalry accoutrements, and were armed with double-barrelled Victoria carbines, which were easily loaded and excellent weapons at point blank range, 100 yards, but required to be elevated at longer distances, and were in this respect much inferior to rifles. A cavalry sword completed their equipment. They were taught, to act mounted and dismounted as occasion required, were admirable skirmishers, and had often proved their good qualities in the field; but unfortunately were not always to be trusted, a portion of them having been detected, during the last war, in the act of going over to the enemy. For this reason, and on account of the enormous expense incurred by the English government in the equipment of so large a force, equal in strength to at least three of our cavalry regiments, they have been disbanded, and as a corps are no longer in existence, their duties being entrusted to a numerous body of mounted police, the colony having now undertaken to protect itself.

On my arrival I lost no time in reporting myself to the colonel of my regiment, Sir Henry Somerset, to whom I was presented in due form. He was a fine specimen of an old soldier, frank and loyal in his bearing, and the *beau ideal* of a cavalry officer of the *old regime*. He had served at Waterloo as a subaltern in the 11th Hussars, and had made himself conspicuous in the different Kaffir campaigns by his bravery and intimate knowledge of the country, and of the bush tactics so necessary in that exceptional warfare. He was a fine looking old man, a regular *vieux d'Afrique,* his bronzed complexion and fine features well contrasted with his large moustache which, with his hair, was snowy white. He had a fine seat on a horse, and when mounted on his white charger, was quite a picture. At the same time his natural kindness of disposition, and the care he always displayed for the comfort and welfare of the officers under his command, in whom he seemed to take an almost fatherly interest, made him quite beloved in the regiment. Many a careless sub has he saved from scrapes and difficulties by his judicious management. He would, for instance, always make it convenient to bring an officer who had been left too long on outpost duty into headquarters, and on the other hand, should one have been imprudent enough to get into debt, or become entangled in some foolish attachment at headquarters, he would contrive to send him off to some distant command, where the opportunity would be given to get over his folly, or to retrench.

As a griffin I was naturally a prey to many a practical joke on the part of my more seasoned comrades. I had not long to wait. The first time I was put on duty as orderly officer was turned to account as follows: I was strutting in all the panoply of sword and feathers into the barracks at midday stables, when a waggish captain came running up to remind me that it was a part of my duty, as orderly officer of the day, to mount my charger and escort the mess cart which was taking up a supply of wine to the colonel's house to ensure its safe arrival. This onerous duty I performed to the astonishment of the mess servant, who was in charge of the equipage. Before I actually reached the hall door, however, I was met by the colonel himself, who had *twigged* my approach from his dining room windows and came out smiling and suspecting mischief. He had evidently much ado to keep his gravity, when touching the peak of my *shako,* I reported the safe arrival of my convoy.

"Ah," said he with an internal chuckle, "those wicked dogs have been hoaxing you, have they? Come in and have a glass of wine and don't be annoyed. You youngsters must expect a little chaffing."

I had now to set about providing myself with horses. These we had to buy at our own cost, our complement including first and second charger and *bat* or packhorse. The hardship of it was that although equipped and mounted as cavalry, with an expensive uniform in addition to the cost of our mounts averaging about £100, we only received infantry pay, and were in fact in a most anomalous position, being neither cavalry nor infantry, or as it is more expressively than elegantly termed, *"neither fish, flesh, fowl, nor good red herring."* Our allowances were raised just before I left the regiment, but not until continual complaints had obliged the authorities to do something to mitigate the evils of our position.

My waggish brother in arms' next exploit was kindly to assist me with a first charger, which being unable to ride himself (as it was a high-spirited and unmanageable brute with an incurable habit of rearing), he was delighted to be rid of and pocket the £50 which I paid him for it. It was a handsome well-bred looking chestnut, and I was very proud of my bargain, until I found out his amiable propensities. He had a habit of bolting out of the riding school, and, getting the bit between his teeth, would run clean away with me back to his stable, and was not particular about charging a stone building if it came in his way, and in this manner, one day gave me a tremendous *purl*, grazing off one half of my moustache which was in a promising state. This was the more cruel as it was the object of much care and anxiety on my part; our position as mounted men allowing us to indulge in this hirsute appendage, the more precious as it was at that time denied to our less fortunate infantry companions. I was horrified one day at witnessing my charger rear up and fall over backwards upon my groom, who remained in the saddle, and I naturally expected that he would be smashed utterly, but to my intense relief he managed to extricate himself unhurt. Strange to say, I afterwards witnessed another instance of a similar lucky escape on a race course in the interior, where a horse reared completely over in the same manner with an inebriated settler on his back who never quitted the saddle, but actually, when his horse struggled to his feet again, came up to the surface still in his seat smiling affably and without a scratch. I can only attribute this to the presence of some inequality in the ground, which must have relieved the pressure. The chestnut was an incorrigible rearer. I got so accustomed at last to his vagaries that when he reared beyond a certain point (we must draw the line somewhere, as the barber said in *Chuzzlewit*), I used to take my feet out of the stirrup and dropping quietly off his back, pull his head down and remount him. I was fortunate enough to get rid of him eventually to a horse breeder of Cradock, who took a fancy to him for breeding purposes. I got the same money as I gave, luckily indeed (as it afterwards proved), for the horse got fever in the feet and went dead lame to the disgust of his purchaser, who was always under the impression that I had taken him in with an unsound animal. This was however not the case, as he was all right when I sold him.

Our riding-school was marked out on the side of a hill near the barracks in the open air, there being no building available for the purpose, and here we were initiated into the mysteries of the double ride and the usual schooling. Our riding master, Salis, was a fine soldierly-looking man, and had been wounded in our encounter with the insurgent Boers at the so-called battle of Boem Platts, where he was disabled by a bullet from one of their long *roers* which shattered his elbow. He was dismounted at the time and was on the point of being despatched, when he fortunately succeeded in rousing the better feelings of the Boer, by reminding him in Dutch that he had a *vrow und kinder* (wife and children) awaiting his return, and *"as one touch of nature makes the whole world kin,"* the family-loving Dutchman was touched at an appeal which came home so forcibly, and stayed his hand.

Salis had been an old dragoon, and was afterwards made riding-master at Maidstone, a post for which he was eminently fitted by his excellent *hand* and temper; but he never recovered the proper use of his left arm, and always carried it in a sling, and had a nervous habit when perplexed of pulling at his fingers, as if he were trying to straighten them. He was lately promoted to be paymaster of the regiment; and it was always a sure sign that there was nothing to be got out of him when he began pulling his fingers, which always led up to the reluctant exclamation: "But, my dear fellow, where are the funds?" uttered in such a plaintive tone, that we hadn't the heart to press him. He was an excellent instructor, and I never saw him lose his temper, and he had, at times, some awkward customers in the shape of pupils to deal with. There was the clumsy youngster with no hand, whose horse was always going *disunited*, and leading off with the wrong leg; the round thighed pupil who invariably rolled off at the word trot, but got up again smiling; and the wag, who when told to ride upon the *bridoon*, retorted that he preferred the saddle. But nothing ever put him out. He had been a pupil of Angelo, and taught us fencing in his odd moments for the love of the thing, and a more obliging and at the same time exact paymaster there could not be.

We were sorry, indeed, when he gave up the riding-school and gave place to a burly dragoon of the plunger type, who exasperated his h's in the most fearful manner, and told us to "*happly* the haids," informed us that we rode "'orrible bad;" and was immediately christened "tea-rot," as that was his peculiar manner of giving that word of command. Possibly this was by way of a caution, like the old Devonshire sergeant-major of yeomanry cavalry who, when drilling his men in the sword-exercise, used to preface his instructions with the admonition: "When I says dra', *don't* dra'! But when I says swurds, hout wie 'em!!" He was a good-natured fellow, but I am afraid he found us rather spoiled by his predecessor.

The regiment, as a rule, was well-horsed. The remounts were mostly purchased at Swellendam and the breeding districts near Cape Town, the regulation price given being limited to £25, which was considered a good price at the Cape for a trooper. They were wiry animals, capable of undergoing great fatigue, seldom more than 14-2 in height, and rather low in the shoulder, and drooping too much in the quarter for beauty; but were thoroughly useful animals, and we performed great distances with them at times, the usual method of travelling being to ride one horse and lead another, to which they were well accustomed. We generally rode a twelve miles stage, and then off saddled and let them have a roll, which they did as a matter of course as soon as they were unharnessed. The dustier the ground, the better they were pleased. This was nearly as good to them as a feed of corn, for they seemed to get up as fresh as ever after it. A major of ours, who was a lightweight, used to ride into headquarters from his outpost at King William's Town, a distance of 85 miles, in a day, when we gave a ball at Graham's Town, and would think nothing of it; and Sir Harry Smith once rode up from Cape Town to Graham's Town, a good 500 miles, over an infamous road, in six days.

The horses had a terrible habit of bucking at times, which-manoeuvre they performed in the usual fashion by suddenly springing up into the air, with all four feet off the ground, their heads being previously planted well down between their fore legs, at the same time crooking their backs into an arch. This was difficult to sit; and to make matters worse, without giving you time to recover your equilibrium, they only reached the ground once more, to take a fresh spring, which usually had the effect of getting you a little more off the perpendicular. If that was not effectual, they commenced bucking round in circles, in a series of bounds, which generally ended the matter by shooting the rider out of the saddle with more or less force upon the top of his head. It was possible to sit the two or three first bucks, but if the brute went on, you were bound to come to grief. I scarcely ever saw the man who could sit a persevering bucker, and if once they succeeded in throwing a rider they would generally repeat the experiment on every practicable occasion. It seemed to be necessary to get their heads down to perform this feat, and the only chance of preventing it, was to hold their heads well up, but there was seldom time to manage this. I certainly heard of one determined *sticker* who boasted that he used to ride a bucker to keep himself in practice. But I never fell in with him, and am inclined to be sceptical on the subject.

We had some queer ones amongst the troopers. I remember one determined brute who could not be ridden, and so was relegated to carry the post bags (we had a frontier post party, consisting of a corporal and two men who went round the outposts), and it was always a sight to see him start. He got at last into the habit of throwing himself on the ground when he was saddled up; and I have seen him do so with such violence that his body remained literally balanced on the cross-bars which projected at the top of the wooden pack-saddle, with all four legs in the air. He was at last sold as incurably vicious. The horses were mostly entire, which made them sometimes very unmanageable. They fought terribly at night, and used to awaken us often with their angry screams, biting each other dreadfully in these encounters. It was no very enjoyable occupation for the stable guard, who had to make his way into their stalls at night, to separate them and tie up the assailants which had contrived to break their strong *reims* and walk about, like the Irishman at Donnybrook, who amused himself by strolling outside the booth and cracking all the skulls of his unfortunate compatriots who were leaning against the canvas covering. As we can imagine the state of mind enjoyed by the recipients of his ill-timed pleasantry, so the kind of retaliation the loose troopers brought upon themselves at the heels of their offended mates can be judged.

Chapter 5

Personal Reminiscences

Baron Jack, as someone appropriately termed our dear old Colonel, who had a most lordly mediaeval way of doing all kinds of things on his own responsibility, was always ready to help us in our schemes for amusement; and, on one occasion, actually sent down the whole of our military band, bag and baggage, to the mouth of the Cowie (where we had improvised a picnic on a large scale) to provide us with dance music. Here they stayed, much to their delight and our own, for a whole week, and here, having pitched our tents on a pretty farm belonging to a jolly Scotch doctor, named Campbell, we had a fine time of it; the old boy riding down himself sometimes to have a look at us. We had plenty of visitors, and many of the Graham Town *belles trekked* down with their families in ox-wagons, and we footed it on the turf in great style.

These African rivers run through beautiful scenery, well wooded with sloping grassy banks and park-like glades, but are scarcely ever navigable, as the tide silts up huge sand bars at the mouths, leaving only a small *embouchure* beneath, through which the river finds its way to the sea. They will never be practicable for trade until the colonial government gets rid of its apathy, and brings engineering science to bear upon the matter by throwing out substantial piers, which would have the effect of diverting the tides and allow the streams to clear themselves, and by force of the current carry the accumulation of sand away as fast as it is deposited.

A speculative member of the legislative chamber bought up the land about the Cowie mouth under the idea that it would remunerate him handsomely some day when it becomes an important harbour; and even went so far as to issue a gorgeous prospectus faced with an imposing coloured illustration of "Cowie Harbour," as he would like to see it, with crowds of shipping, boats busily employed in landing their cargoes and yachts sailing in and out, the whole making a very effective picture, if, like the Marchioness, you *made believe* a good deal. This prospectus was issued many years since, but the Cowie Harbour is, as far as I know, still *in futuro*. In the meanwhile the honourable member got a good deal of prospective credit for his foresight, and was often heard to declare that the "Cowie 'arbour was his 'obby." I am afraid he dropped something more valuable than his h's in the speculation.

About this time Colonel Somerset was made a Major-General and K.C.B. The consequence was that we lost him. The command of the regiment now devolved on Colonel S., who was away on leave at the time far in the interior on a sporting tour. Reports had come down of the number of large game he had demolished, and hippopotami were, we were told, becoming scarce on this account. I was quite prepared, therefore, to see a mighty hunter of the Gordon Cumming type, *"full of strange oaths and bearded like the pard."* Full of strange oaths I must confess he was, but there the resemblance ended. He was a very little man, about five feet four, with a sharp-featured bronzed face, and a high-dried look about him, and had not an ounce of superfluous fat on his frame. Though small in person, he was large in gesture, walked like a heavy dragoon, as if his limbs were inconveniently large for him, and seldom opened his mouth without an expletive. One peculiarity of his was that, without intending to be witty, he made use of such odd phrases and incongruous metaphors,

Indeed, his mouth he scarce could ope,
But out of it there fell a trope,

47

that even in his vituperative moments, which were numerous, he was irresistibly ludicrous, and sent us off into convulsions of suppressed laughter.

I shall give a few instances of these peculiarities, but I wish I could give an idea of the strange attitudes and extravagant gestures that accompanied them, and added so much to their zest.

Imagine the regiment assembled upon the parade ground preparatory to a general inspection by the commander of the forces, a terrible martinet of the old school of whom we stood in wholesome awe. The different troops have been told off and formed into, squadrons. The band, conspicuous by its white horses and gay uniforms, has fallen in on the flank, and we are in readiness to march off to the drill ground, where the inspecting general will be found to receive us, as the gallant little colonel comes ambling up on his roman-nosed charger. I must premise that he is an old infantry officer, and not being strong in equestrianism prefers the sober reflective style of animal to the barbed steed; one that has no particular desire to say *ha! ha!* to the shouting of the captains. Imagine this bizarre little warrior, habited in a scantily fashioned hussar uniform of antique pattern, once invisible, now turned by the united efforts of sun and wind to a very visible, green, and tight even for his spare frame, wearing a tall *shako* surmounted by a flowing plume, the *lines* of which, instead of falling "in pleasant places" gracefully pendant on his shoulder, are tied up out of the way in a clumsy knot at the top. (This head-dress, by the way, was a source of unmitigated misery to Colonel S. The fact was, he had led such a free-and-easy life in the *veldt*, in which he had spent so much of his sporting life, that the restraint of a tight uniform was very irksome to him, and the *shako* especially so, from the unaccommodating nature of its material and the weight of its super-incumbent plume. I have seen him after attending a court-martial snatch it off his head, and kick it viciously all round the room when he had a difficulty in adjusting it.)

The parade is now called to attention, as the colonel passes down the ranks on his tour of inspection, stopping now and again to find fault, and objurgating the object of his discontent with the most grotesque personal abuse; now roaring out to an unfortunate sergeant (who coming from a smart Lancer regiment is in the habit of making the most of himself), "Now Mister Sergeant Brown, don't let's have any of those George the Fourth coronation airs, if *you* please" (the sergeant was making his horse prance, and has something of the air of Peter the Great on his pedestal); *anon* informing a wretched private, whose forage cap is not well set, that his head looks "like a thimble with a button on the top," and winding up with a shriek of disgust at finding that the medical packhorse is missing from parade. Then what a rush of sergeants and orderlies to search for the recreant animal. What a shower of unnecessary oaths when he does not turn up, and we are detained until the hour of rendezvous is past. Imagine the feeling of relief when it is discovered that the horse has been on the ground all the time, hidden away behind one of the troops, the discovery being made by the colonel himself in his wanderings, with the triumphant exclamation, "Here's the packhorse! Here's the medical packhorse! Rained down from Heaven, by Gad!"

I was attending at the orderly room one day when the little man was busily employed in writing despatches, and the sergeant-major ushered in a rough sailor-like man in civilian garments, who stood nervously fumbling with an old tarpaulin hat and looking about him sheepishly. Presently the little colonel looked up from his writing and discerned him.

"Well, what do you want?" he ejaculated so suddenly that the poor man was quite startled.

"If you please, colonel," said the man humbly, "I wanted to know if I could be enlisted to serve in the Cape Corps?"

"You, you!" shrieked the colonel, eyeing *him* savagely. "Why every hair in your head would make a toothpick. Get out!"

The astonished applicant (who was certainly rather antique) took the hint.

There was a tradition in the regiment that he once sentenced a private who would not get his hair cut short enough to please him (this was always a serious cause of offence), to be confined to barracks for the remainder of his natural life, and to have his hair cut every two hours! But this, I am afraid, was exaggeration. His sayings and doings would fill a volume, which would, I believe, be unique of its kind. But with all these eccentricities he was a highly educated agreeable man in society, and was a thorough sportsman. His good qualities were his own, and his foibles the result of old associations, and the fashion of an obsolete regime which is happily becoming more and more rare, and is fast giving way before the increase of refinement and good feeling of the present day.

Behold in the person of the major-general another type, *the old cavalry plunger*, who may be characterised as a species of military *Bombastes Furioso*. He was a terrible martinet, great indeed on the subject of shoulder-straps and pipe clay. A perfect antithesis-to the little colonel, he is mighty of stature and much padded of person. His gray moustache, dyed a coal black, is waxed into long points. He positively swells with importance. His prominent gray eyes, set *à fleur de la tête* in a rubicund visage, are empurpled by the united effects of good living and a high military stock. I don't know that he had seen any important service, but he was great in matters of detail,. and woe to the unfortunate officer who couldn't tell off-handed the name and age of every man and horse in his troop, their regimental numbers, personal history and antecedents. He led the little colonel a terrible life of it; sending for him on all occasions, and having us out for drill and inspection continually, and making our lives generally uncomfortable.

As our duties on service were principally confined to skirmishing, a style of fighting in which the regiment was very adroit, we could not see the *cui bono* of this incessant parade in a savage country like the Cape, especially under the command of an officer who had no experience in bush warfare; and, as most of us were old campaigners, we were sometimes rather out of patience.

He sat his horse like a pair of scissors, with his toes well turned out, which was the old fashioned cavalry seat, the instruction being to avoid *clinging at the knees*, as they termed it; and in consequence, they rode entirely by balance, and if a stirrup gave way, or rough ground had to be traversed, they were quite dependent upon it. If a man with a seat of this kind was put on a plain saddle, he was quite helpless in a case of difficulty. We had an instance of this in one of our officers, who had served in the ranks, and had actually attained the grade of sergeant in an English cavalry regiment, and yet acknowledged that he had no seat on a plain saddle.

The present military seat, which in fact is the hunting position with the knees tight to the saddle flaps, and the legs taking their natural place, the feet not thrust quite so far into the stirrup as in hunting, but far enough to afford a good hold, differing again from the old seat, where the point of the toe was only just allowed to touch it, is now all that can be desired, and at the same time neat and soldierly. Our old riding-master Salis, who had a long experience in the country, although he was particular enough in the school, did not, for instance, insist on our *bumping* the saddle, as it is termed, but allowed us to rise in the stirrup on the march, as he said it was too fatiguing for men and horses in a hot climate. And there is no doubt that if some of our depot pipe clay notions were kept in abeyance when our troops are employed in foreign service, it would be of great advantage.

I remember at the commencement of the Kaffir war of '51, a very fine officer, but unused to bush fighting, marching his men thirty miles a day in full dress and in heavy marching order; the consequence of which was that they were falling out continually, half fainting from fatigue. Before he had been long in the country the whole regiment was clad in civilian costume. In these cases an ounce of practice is worth a pound of theory. The Cape Rifle Regiment was rough and ready, and any attempt to make it into a crack cavalry regiment would have been not only impossible, but totally unnecessary. So patent were these facts to common sense, that in the Kaffir war of '51 nearly the whole army were habited *en bourgeois*—loose handkerchiefs taking the place of black stocks and soft felt wide-awakes of *shakos*; a change by which the men had the free use of their limbs and skirmished all the better. The officers initiated a comfortable style of patrol jacket, which was, I believe, also adopted in the

Abyssinian war under Sir Garnet Wolseley. The tight stock itself is an abomination. Let anyone who is sceptical try it with the thermometer at 110°, and see how he likes it! It is now, I believe, modified to a certain extent, but was, I have no doubt, a fruitful source of apoplexy, misnamed *coup de soleil*, in olden times.

What chance, for instance, has a man buttoned up to the throat and encumbered with heavy accoutrements, carrying sixty rounds of ammunition (the Kaffirs used to call them pack oxen), against a naked savage in the bush, in a skirmish? To begin with, the tangled bush presents such insuperable impediments to his progress that he is obliged to keep in the open, whilst his foe can slip through the most intricate scrub, and deliver his fire under cover, in fact *walk round him*. It resolves itself into this: that the fewer obstructions we put in his way the better for the soldier.

The general was a heavy feeder, and a capital judge of wine. I never shall forget how he got the best of us over a case of claret, which was part of a consignment of wine which we had ordered out from England. He was dining at our mess one evening, when the first bottle was decanted, and after gulping down a glass of it, in approved connoisseur fashion, held it up to the light and shook his head, giving us his opinion that it was "corked, yes, decidedly corked." Then ensued the conflict of opinion usual in such cases; some averring that it was, and others that it was not. The heavy weight of the general's dictum gained the day, and it was replaced by another wine which was pronounced satisfactory. We actually discovered, some time afterwards, that the general had sent someone to make a bid for the depreciated wine, and had bought the whole of it. It was in point of fact perfectly good and sound, and, if I recollect aright, was considered some of the best produced at his table on subsequent occasions. It was never satisfactorily settled who was to blame in the matter; but some of the amateur wine-tasters were rather chary of giving their opinion of corked wine for some time afterwards.

When I first joined the regiment, in the year 1850, the days of military examinations, as all the world knows, had not yet come to vex the souls of fearful subalterns. Strange as it may appear, the educational standard was higher at that time in the regiment than it ever was after their introduction. Nearly all the old officers joined us at a more advanced age than was allowed in the *line*, and most of them, like myself, had seen something of the world before they entered the service. I must candidly confess that the candidates who came in under the new system did not impress us much with their superiority. If they did make their *entree* full of knowledge, they were very modest, and did not make any show of it. Their spelling, for instance, was occasionally open to objection. I trust I shall not be thought invidious if I give a little episode *a propos* of the subject.

One of our lately joined subs, who had safely accomplished this intellectual ordeal, was writing a note one morning which his soldier servant was to take into the town. A wicked brother officer looking over his shoulder (knowing, I suppose, the purport of his epistle, which, by-the-bye, was no excuse for his doing so) read as follows: "Sir, please send me some *hare* oil by the bearer, yours, &c." This wicked individual, who was fond of a practical joke, said nothing at the time, but later on, when the cloth had been removed after mess, and the servants had retired, suddenly addressed his companions:

"Oh, by-the-bye," said he, "I've got such a capital story to tell you," and he began relating the history of the epistolary composition, fixing his eye upon the unfortunate culprit, who immediately got crimson in the face, suspecting danger.

"And how do you think he spelt *hair*?" said he, looking round at us, who were all anxiety to hear the *denouement*, "*h, a, i, r*," he solemnly ejaculated, dwelling upon each letter.

"I'll be hanged if I did," said the excited subaltern, in a voice of thunder; "I spelt it *h, a, r, e*."

It was a long time before he could look a hare in the face after that, I can assure you.

I hope the reader will not think that I am getting into what Douglas Jerrold calls "my anecdotage;" but I must, in justice to the *erudite candidates*, recall one more little instance of an *unimaginative man*," who had *not* passed his examination. I wonder whether the *system* would have done anything for him! Poor

Paddy S.! he was as plucky a fellow as ever burnt powder; but, as I say, his fault was—a want of imagination. He was not what is called a *reading man*; but time will hang heavy on one's hands at an outpost, and Paddy came lounging into my quarters one day, and asked me if I would lend him a book? I told him to look over my shelf and help himself to what he fancied. After making a survey, he walked off with *The Arabian Nights*—a book I am still very fond of. Paddy kept it for a fortnight, and I was afraid that he had lost it, when he brought it back one morning and threw it down quite contemptuously on the table.

"Well, what do you think of it? "said I.

"Why," he said, scratching his *shock* head, "I don't believe a word of it."

CHAPTER 6

Fort Brown

The different troops of which the Cape Mounted Rifles were composed, were scattered all over the country on outpost duty; and as good shooting was generally to be found at these stations, it was a very popular service. I had not been long at Graham's Town when I was sent out, in my turn of duty, to Fort Brown, in charge of the L troop, to which I belonged, in the absence of the captain, who had gone home on leave. As it was only some twenty miles distant on the Great Fish River, I had the advantage of receiving frequent visits from my brother officers, who rode out to see me and joined in my expeditions.

The road to this fort passed through the beautiful Ecca Valley, by a path cut in the precipitous face of the pass, whose sides were clothed with *spek-boem* (elephant bush), and all kinds of flowering shrubs. The road looked down a declivity of some 200 feet, and had been worn in places into a perfect staircase of boulders by successive torrents of tropical rain, and was quite impracticable to any other vehicle than a Cape wagon. The edge facing the precipice had no kind of parapet, and the dangerous nature of the pass was brought into still greater prominence by the fact that the debris of an ox wagon still lay broken up in minute particles at the bottom of the valley, where it had evidently gone down bodily with its span of oxen. The pass was, however, very beautiful. *Convolvuli* ran over the bushes in rich clusters, the star-shaped jessamine with its pink undersides, and the magnificent *Strellitzea Regina* nourished; whilst the scarlet geraniums attained a height of ten or twelve feet amidst the thick bush.

The outposts, of which Fort Brown was an example, formed in fact a perfect chain of forts, placed in commanding positions over the whole area of the frontier, and were mostly stone buildings, solidly constructed, square in form, the walls being loopholed for musketry; each fort containing accommodation for a certain number of mounted men and a detachment of infantry. Some of them were very isolated, and their garrisons, at times, put to great straits for supplies; the communication being difficult in time of war from the impracticable nature of the bush, with which they were surrounded, which was so tangled and full of evergreen shrubs and succulent plants that it was quite impervious to fire, and could only be partially cleared.

The forts were constructed by that scientific corps, the Royal Engineers, some of whom made themselves conspicuous by their want of practical knowledge, and perpetrated the most astounding blunders. In one fort, for instance, the staircases leading to the upper floors were absolutely left out of the plan and had to be afterwards added. In another, which was intended to hold a big gun, the doorway had to be enlarged after it was constructed, as there was not sufficient space to admit of its entrance; and tradition proclaims that a certain engineer officer handed his name down to an admiring posterity by the peculiar manner in which he carried out the order to *muffle oars* on a river expedition at Buffalo Mouth. On this occasion the men, finding the oars difficult to manage, discerned that the blades had been carefully enveloped in sacking instead of the rowlocks, so that they made rather more noise than usual as they were drawn out of the water. From this circumstance he earned the sobriquet of "Muffles" from that time forth. In other words, an engineer officer may be quite capable of solving the most difficult problem in Euclid, and, at the same time, from the want of a little practical knowledge, may perpetrate blunders that would disgrace the commonest carpenter.

Fort Brown was built upon an open tract of country near the banks of the Great Fish River, which was here spanned by a well-constructed wooden bridge of imposing height and dimensions. This river, like most African streams, is subject to great fluctuations. I have seen it in dry seasons so narrow in places that one might jump over it without difficulty; and again, in times of flood, twenty and thirty feet deep, running with a powerful current that rendered it quite impassable. In these dangerous watercourses the banks are very high, with sides scarped by the force of the stream. The fording places only occur at long intervals, so that, when crossing in a flood, it is not always easy to hit them off, and if once carried down the stream by the strength of the current you have very little chance of escaping an accident. A colonel of the 60th Rifles and several officers were drowned in this manner during the war.

The best way of crossing a flooded river is to adopt the Kaffir plan of taking off some way up the stream, to allow for driftage. I have seen old settlers undress themselves completely before mounting their horses, and carry their clothes in a bundle on their heads on the chance of a capsize. The stirrups should be crossed over the pommel of the saddle and the horse allowed to have his head, guiding him by the snaffle, and in difficult cases it is better to relieve him of your weight altogether by floating alongside of him, only guiding his head in the proper direction.

The Great Fish River flows through very fine scenery, at times bordered by impenetrable bush and tangled vegetation of all descriptions, again winding under lofty mountains or *krantzes* of basaltic rock beautifully variegated with foliage, the thickets affording shelter to swarms of animal and insect life, giving rise on a still evening to a perfect babble of sound, amidst which the plaintive *coo* of the ringdove, the incessant chirp of the cicada, the twittering of birds, and the hoarse croaking of the bull-frogs, are pre-eminent. These frogs are wonderfully sonorous and demonstrative in South Africa. On one occasion after a storm, their musical croakings were so resonant and horn-like, that I remained for some time under the impression that I was listening to distant music. The occasion I allude to was a joyous one for the frog world. I was riding into the pretty village of Somerset, on my way from Graaf Reinet with a mounted escort, when we were overtaken by a terrific storm. Only those accustomed to tropical countries can form an idea of the grandeur of these outbreaks. The thunder cracks as if the vault of heaven were rending asunder, and the lightning literally covers the ground in huge sheets, and seems completely to envelop one; whilst tiny rivulets become foaming, irresistible torrents. Then is the African frog in his glory. They are most mysterious creatures. I have often stood over a mud bank and peered about in vain to discern their whereabouts, whilst their harsh croak resounded seemingly at my very feet, their hiding places being at the same time quite invisible.

I often angled in the Great Fish River, where I caught mullet and eels in great abundance, frequently filling my basket with the former. There are great numbers of iguana, a large waterlizard of a dark hue speckled with white, which attains a length of five feet. It would often startle me by its sudden plunge off the bank when I disturbed it. A little blear-eyed old man, who had located himself in a hut just outside, the fort, where he gained a precarious livelihood by stuffing birds and doing odd-jobs for the settlers near, used to cut off the iguanas' tails and cook them. Finding him busily employed in preparing this recondite dish one day as I was passing, he induced me to taste it. I found it very white and delicate, with a slight resemblance to chicken, but rather insipid. This old man had served in the Royal Navy in his youth, where, according to his own account, he had distinguished himself principally by deserting from the different vessels to which he was appointed, which he evidently considered a thing to be chuckled over. Leaving his last ship at Table Bay, and being fond of adventure, he had turned trapper, and occupied himself with elephant shooting and trading in the interior, and spun me many an interesting yarn about his exploits. He had evidently been in the habit of roughing it considerably, and as misery is said to make us acquainted with strange bedfellows, so necessity had made him acquainted with strange viands.

Apropos of this subject, he used to narrate with great glee, how he once entertained two English travellers who passed his hut one evening, and being benighted asked him for shelter. He bid them welcome, and as they made themselves comfortable by his wood fire, one of them remarked what a nice smell the *pol eu feu,* which was warming up the old man's supper, gave out.

"Ah," said he; "I should think it was good! You shall taste it presently."

The cooking was at last consummated, and the travellers sat down with famished appetites to the savoury mess.

"If there's anything I have a fancy for it's eels," said one of them after he had swallowed a good portion of the dish.

"Them's not heels!" said the old man, "them's snakes!"

Imagine the tableau!

Under his tuition I became expert in setting up birds, of which there were many beautiful varieties. Conspicuous amongst them were the little crested. kingfisher, a perfect gem of colour, several varieties of sugar bird, a species allied to the humming-birds or *hoverers,* which were constantly to be seen flying restlessly over the aloe blossom, the orange-throated lark, the beautiful blue jay, and the Kaffir finch, whose black and white plumage and red throat were set off by his long streaming tail, the feathers of which are so prolonged that they droop into a perfect arch, and when flying nearly overbalance him.

The sandy plain on which the fort was situated was covered with stunted *karoo* bush and full of Duyker *gries*-buck, and bush-buck. Two kinds of hares frequented the plains: the larger kind, grey, furred like our rabbit, and a small red mountain' species, better eating than the former, which was scarcely considered fit for the table on account of its scavenging propensities, as it was in the habit of feeding upon the refuse of the fort, and was distrusted accordingly.

I found on the plains enormous land tortoises and many strange *ferae-naturae.* Not the least singular of these was the spring hare, or *spring hasen* of the colonists, a singular little animal of the *Gerboa* species, about the size of an ordinary hare, which burrows in the sand, and only emerges at night to feed, and which when wounded emits a most peculiar scream like a penny trumpet. The sound so startled me one day when I was out shooting, that having picked one up which I had hit, I was fain to let it fall again and escape in my astonishment. For game birds we had the grey partridge and the Cape pheasant; the latter, which is a species of jungle fowl, being almost tail-less, the plumage alone being pheasant-like, but wanting altogether the brilliant colouring. The prevailing tints are limited to the sombre-brown and yellow-streaked feathers found on the back of the real bird, the head at the same time being more fowl-like, with its red wattles, and the legs clumsy, crimson coloured, and furnished with double spurs. It is much given to running in the thick scrub, from whence it is difficult to drive it, and never rises on the wing unless compelled, when it mounts like the English pheasant, and presents a very easy mark to sportsmen. We had a sprinkling of red wing, but the game grey partridge was more predominant. To find these we used to make excursions to the rocky ranges of Botha's Hill, which dominated the wide flats contiguous to Graham's Town, where we had good sport, as the birds lay well in the rocky ground and our pointers came into play.

The great drawback to the use of pointers was the want of water, the prevalence of thorns, and the quantity of snakes. Of all the numerous varieties of the latter, the puff adder is the most dangerous. It is a hideous reptile, of a faded brown colour, with a swollen body and a fatally venomous bite, and so sluggish in its movements that it seldom gets out of the way, and one is apt to tread upon it in the long grass, in which case it invariably retaliates. The dogs point it, happily, just as they would game (no doubt from its strong odour), and one frequently walks up to them ready for a shot only to discover one of these loathsome looking reptiles, coiled up ready to make its deadly spring. The satisfaction of anticipating its murderous intentions by blowing its head off with a charge of shot is very great.

There is a nasty thorn called the *doublegee*, which forms a triangle, and presents a point upwards whichever way it falls. This thorn runs into the unfortunate dog's feet, and quite disables him. They have indeed to be continually extracted. Water, again, is very difficult to find in the dry season, and it is necessary, when partridge shooting in the interior, to take a supply in barrels in your wagon for the pointers, or they invariably get knocked up. The colonists are very improvident in the matter of water supply. Only here and there, at rare intervals, is anything in the shape of a dam to be found, and the small streams, upon which the farms are dependent, are either torrents or dried up into a succession of pools often failing altogether. Yet no precaution is taken to save the, at times, abundant supply of water; the settlers, in time of drought, simply trekking away with all his stock to some more favoured region, until his home supply is once more recruited.

In the category of strange creatures to be found in this district, I must not omit the ant-bear, or *aard-vark* (earth pig), which not only inhabits the frontier, but is spread over all parts of the interior, the surface of the ground for miles being completely honeycombed with the holes excavated by the claws of this indefatigable burrower in search of the daily ant-food upon which he subsists. His soft muzzle and innocent calf-like head, with its mild bluish eyes, seem almost disproportionate, set upon his bulky, shapeless body, sparsely covered with scanty bristles. His *porcine* body, again, is at variance with his formidable claws and broad muscular forearms, which enable him with ease to dig his circular shaft, some two feet in diameter, in the hardest ground, descending vertically to a depth of three or four feet before it takes its lateral direction. These holes present a formidable obstruction to the hunter, riding after large game, who is frequently rolled over in full career by the sudden subsidence of his horse's fore-legs in one of these dangerous pitfalls.

It was some time before I had the good luck to get even a glimpse of these shy animals. Returning one evening towards dusk to the fort, I was startled by the rush through the low bushes of a nondescript animal, which scuttled away with most uncouth movements, leaving in his trail a perfect shower of earth and pebbles. I fired a snap shot at him as he was disappearing behind the bushes, apparently without effect; but, on passing the spot the next morning, I discovered the head and part of the flesh of an ant-hear hanging on a *speck boem* bush, the rejected spoil of some Kaffir or Hottentot, who had evidently found him dead, and was no doubt making a meal upon the remainder.

Since that time I have had several opportunities of observing the habits of this singular and little known animal. He leaves his shelter only at night, and is extremely shy and sensitive to discovery, making his earth close to the large ant-heaps so numerously distributed over the *veldt*. Here he scrapes a shallow trench in the upper surface, which has the effect of bringing out the ants in great numbers; then, lying extended at full length resting on his fore-paws, he-launches out his prehensile tongue into the cavity,. waiting patiently until it is completely covered with insects before he withdraws it, which manoeuvre he repeats until he is satisfied. (His tongue is provided with two powerful sets of muscles for this purpose.) The ant-bear is sometimes surprised in the open in the day time by the Boers, who hunt him with dogs; in which case, though unprovided with teeth, he defends himself most effectually by striking out on either side with his strong forearms, and tumbles his assailants over right and left, often ripping them up with his dangerous claws. When he has succeeded in running to earth, the Boers try and dig him out of his retreat; but this is no easy matter, as he can make his way underground often more rapidly than they can follow him. They have a way, however, of stopping his progress by stamping upon the ground over his head, or striking it heavily with a pole, which confuses him probably from his uncertainty as to the direction from which danger is to be expected. His flesh is considered fit for table, and, according to the Boers, eats like excellent pork, the crackling being esteemed especially delicious. The Hottentots are particularly fond of it. This curious race, who are now found scattered indifferently over the frontier, it may here be said, originally inhabited the country bordering upon Cape Town, forming a distinct race under its proper chiefs, quite apart from the Kaffirs and Fingoes who inhabit the interior.

CHAPTER 7

The Fingoes

The Fingoes were originally an agglomeration of inferior tribes inhabiting the more remote districts, whom the more warlike Kaffirs had at different times driven before them, and kept in servitude. From this position they were rescued by the English, and located in the colony, where they have since remained, and have, on different occasions, aided us as allies against their inveterate enemies, and by their willing labour and docile habits, done us good service as yeomen. Natives of a hotter climate, they are darker in hue, and show more of the Negro type than the Kaffir, and are not so symmetrical in their proportions as the Amakosoe, whose physical attributes are of a very high order, and who, indeed, often present perfect models of strength and grace. As servants the Fingoes are invaluable to the colonists; that is, such as will take service, and are not unreasonable in their demands. Unlike the Hottentots, who are utterly thriftless and vagabond, they have a turn for saving, and even amass money, which they usually expend in the purchase of an ox-wagon and team, plying as carriers on the main road. On the frontier they are located in large settlements or *kraals*, built near the forts; the principal villages at Fort Peddie and King William's Town containing some 700 or 800 of them with their families. Their huts, built in the same manner as the Kaffirs, of reeds and clay, of a conical shape, are disposed in streets so as to defend their large cattle enclosures in the centre, into which the herds are driven at night for protection. They are useful also as surf men, and may be seen busily employed unloading the boats which ply between the vessels and the shore at Algoa Bay, working away half naked, but always good-tempered and willing.

The Hottentots no longer exist as a people, having become completely absorbed amongst the mixed population of the colony, where they are only to be found as dependants, gaining a precarious living as wagon-drivers, *foer loupers*, servants, or anything that turns up, and are in fact thorough Bohemians, and the most reckless and degraded of mortals. Their complexion is of a sickly parchment hue, and their short, woolly hair grows in little isolated tufts, showing the yellow scalp underneath. Their flat noses, deep, sunken eyes elevated at the angles, projecting lips, and sensual expression, being quite in keeping with their depraved tastes, and proclaiming them at once as among the lowest types of humanity. They are active and energetic, however, in their movements, but dissipate their earnings as soon as gained in the lowest debauchery, men and women often lying about in a senseless state of intoxication. Chastity is a virtue unknown amongst them. Their only redeeming point is their merry disposition. They are fond of a joke, are excellent mimics, and on the road will sing songs round the *outspan* fire, gambling with a dirty pack of cards, or playing on a cracked fiddle, shrieking with laughter, and keeping up an incessant chatter far into the night, for sleep with them is quite a secondary consideration. Tobacco and *Cape smoke*, a detestable kind of white brandy made of peach kernels, are the chief aims of their existence; but they are sociable in their cups. I have seen, more than once, a Hottentot woman emerge from a spirit shop, where, she had been satisfying her own thirst, with her mouth full of brandy, equal portions of which she ejected into the mouths of her companions, who were waiting outside. The Hottentot women, it is generally known, do not require any artificial aids from what are elegantly known in our day as dress improvers. And I was much amused one day when walking in the streets of the capital, to observe one of these creatures strutting in front of two colonial *belles*, who were got up in the latest fashion, triumphantly exclaiming, as she pointed to her own ample endowments, "Dis all real, no sham!"

The Kaffir, on the other hand, is, both physically and intellectually, vastly superior to the Hottentot, averaging five feet nine inches in height, and very finely formed, with features more regular, and the Negro type less prominent. They have the habit (common, I believe, to most savage tribes) of smearing themselves over with a mixture of red clay and grease, which, causes them to appear of a becoming copper colour. They are vegetarians, living almost entirely on Kaffir corn and sour milk left to ferment in skins until it becomes thick, despising it when sweet as unfit for grown men. The women when young are almost pretty, and very graceful, but soon lose their symmetry. They it is who till the ground, sow the corn, and perform all the drudgery, the men occupying themselves with war and the chase, their dignity not allowing them to labour.

When game is scarce, they hunt in large parties, and surround a considerable tract of country, the game, consisting of antelopes of various kinds, interspersed with hares and partridges, is driven by the gradually contracting circle towards the centre, where it is eventually despatched with *knob kerries*, and *assegais*, the former, a long knobbed stick of heavy wood, which they throw with great dexterity, being able to knock down a partridge on the wing at thirty yards.

The use of tobacco is universal, that plant being indigenous; and they are also much addicted to smoking the wild hemp called *dacca*, which they cultivate for the purpose. The smaller leaves of this plant are dried in the sun, and being ground fine, the fumes are inhaled through a pipe, exciting the nervous system frightfully, and more especially affecting the lungs in a most violent manner, the smoker being subjected to violent paroxysms of spasmodic coughing, which eventually leaves him in a stupid dreamy state, accompanied by utter mental and bodily prostration. The Muntatees and other tribes, when unprovided with pipes, have an ingenious method of smoking the *dacca* out of the ground, moistening the earth and stamping it with their naked feet into a stiff clay, they form the stem of the pipe by passing a long curved twig through the soil in a semi-circular direction. The hole is made by enlarging one end where it reaches the surface with the finger; into this they put the lighted *dacca*, and apply their mouths to the other end, each inspiration being accompanied by a draught of water. They take snuff in great quantities, rubbing it into their teeth and gums as well as snuffing it; and they carry a supply of it with them in small gourds grown for the purpose, taking it out with little wooden spoons made to fit into the stopper.

They are all incorrigible thieves, regarding colonial horses and cattle as their legitimate spoil. So continual are their thefts, that the most stringent laws are obliged to be made for the protection of the colonists; the frontier law, requiring that when cattle are stolen, such head man or chief of a *kraal* to which the *spoor* is traced, to carry it on, so as to show that it goes on out of his land on to that of some other person. When the *spoor* is finally traced, a considerable penalty, sometimes double or treble the value of the missing property, is inflicted upon the transgressor; the law considering the owner responsible without reference to the particular thief. This system of plunder has been the cause of innumerable complaints from the colonists, and is generally the indirect cause of our Kaffir wars; the natives being seldom known to attack the white man in his homestead, or to make war upon him to gratify revenge or indulge in the abstract pleasure of murdering, so much as to have some pretext for stealing cattle, or regaining what they or their ancestors have lost in former encounters, and never indeed risk their lives without some immediate prospect of gain.

They are not so much addicted to the use of ardent spirits as many savage nations; but will drink them greedily enough at your expense, the drunkenness being principally found amongst the chiefs, who in times of peace are great beggars. The most powerful will think it no degradation to come into your house and ask for anything he may have taken a fancy to; commencing with a request for an old coat, or a pair of cast-off trousers, and gliding, by an easy and graceful transition, from that to a glass of brandy or wine, *dikpence* (sixpence), or half an inch of tobacco. If under the influence of excitement, you should kick him bodily out of the house, it is ten to one, instead of resenting it, he will, when you meet him on the morrow, say that you hurt him the day before, and beg *dikpence* or a shilling by way of compensation, and at last go off with a threepenny bit to the nearest canteen, perfectly contented.

They are far from deficient in intellect, however, and have shown themselves on various occasions able politicians. At some of the great meetings called together by the governor for the time being, for the purpose of impressing the Kaffir with the justice of some particular measure, which that wily individual does not consider quite so much to his interest, he will listen patiently with seeming conviction until the great man has wound up his discourse with some eloquent peroration, when he will ask some home question or put some sarcastic interpretation upon it, which shows how perfectly he understands the exact merits of the case—sometimes completely nonplussing the wary politician.

"If we your children why not give plenty tobacco and stop fighting poor Kaffir?"

I once heard a hoary-headed Kaffir cry out to Sir Harry Smith, who always appealed to them by this endearing epithet.

CHAPTER 8

The Zulus and Natal

Conspicuous amongst the Kaffir tribes beyond the frontier are the Zulus, who inhabit the country adjoining our settlement of Natal. The district of Natal covers an area of about 20,000 square miles, with a population of 263,000, as estimated in 1807, of whom 250,000 were natives. It is a fine healthy country, the air being dry and clear, averaging about 75° Fahrenheit in summer, and ranging between 62° and 64° in winter. D'Urban, the port, is a dull uninteresting town; but the capital, Pietermaritzberg, 50 miles distant, is a charming place; lying in a valley, surrounded by verdant hills. The river Umsumduzi, its banks enriched with willow trees, which were originally brought from England, and flourish luxuriantly, flows through it, and gives animation to the scene.

The country about Pietermaritzberg gradually slopes from the Drakenberg Mountain to the sea, and the town itself is the residence of the lieutenant-governor with a legislative assembly. Its European inhabitants are composed of Dutch and English. The natives who reside in the colony are subject to a capitation tax of five shillings, which is collected by a magistrate or collector assisted by a force of native police, who are very reliable and efficient. A handsome new bridge spans the river at the entrance to the town. All natives who cross over on their way to the town are obliged to appear clothed, and so strictly is this regulation enforced that they actually, when unprovided, hire clothing for the purpose from their more civilized brethren, who make a decent profit out of the transaction. No sooner do they emerge from the precincts of Pietermaritzberg, however, than the clothes are cast off joyfully, and they once more appear *in puris naturalibus.*

The Zulu Kaffirs are, I think, even taller than the Amakosae, not unfrequently reaching six feet three, and are still more European in feature, the women being very tall of stature and good-looking, but more scantily clothed than their frontier sisters; a necklace of beads, or a circlet of the same round their waists, being considered sufficient adornment.

Besides their covering of dressed skins of beasts, the men wear an apron of cats' tails, strung together and fastened round the waist, which has rather a picturesque effect upon their copper-coloured skins; and they have a singular custom of plastering a circle of hard clay round their heads, the hair being shaved off close to the scalp for this purpose, the chiefs indulging in three or four such circles. The remaining hair, like the Amakosae, is worked up on grand occasions into a stiff hedge with red clay and grease, and further ornamented with feathers. When desirous of creating an extra favourable impression upon their lady friends, especially at the fetes or grand dances, on which occasion they assemble in crowds even to the number of thousands, they fasten live birds of gay plumage to their necks, which as they dance present a most bizarre appearance. The young men wear no clothing until they have attained to manhood.

The Zulus anoint their bodies with castor oil expressed from the berry of the castor oil plant, which grows here in profusion, and paint themselves over with red clay, and have a grotesque habit of boring their ears and inserting small wooden boxes or pieces of antelope horn, in which they carry their snuff, which destroys the shape and symmetry of the organ, giving it a limp dog's eared appearance, which is anything but becoming. They are sober and self-denying, and seem to have quite a horror of a drunkard, and are altogether a fine temperate race, industrious and cheerful, not at all averse to labour, and may be seen busily employed on the sugar plantations, and are indeed far superior to any imported labour. The Indian *coolie* system has turned out rather a failure, as the men are incomparably inferior in physique to the Zulu. The Zulu Kaffir is as naturally cleanly and decent in his habits as the *coolies* are deficient, and he has a great contempt for the latter, his hut presenting a striking contrast in this particular.

The country abounds in game of various sorts. Like the frontier Kaffirs the Zulus hunt in large parties, surrounding the game; each turning round and delivering his *assegais* with wonderful dexterity as he passes the game brought to bay in the centre. Immediately around Pietermaritzberg the game is comparatively scarce, consisting principally of the small *Ipite Bok*, a graceful little antelope, hyenas, wild pig, and leopards; but as the sportsman advances further towards the Drakenberg and Umzumkulu he meets with the rhinoceros, hippopotamus, lions, giraffes, and all the various species of large animals.

To assist the Zulus in the chase, large dogs of the lurcher breed are employed. They are held in leashes until required, and are very swift and staunch. Strange to say, English dogs will not live many months in Natal, but they are often imported for the purpose of crossing with the native dogs, especially the bulldog, which supplies the pluck so deficient in the native animal, and makes the latter most valuable for hunting purposes. Cattle and goats thrive well in the *veldt*, but sheep not at all; and the Zulus' wealth consists in large herds of the former, which are the usual medium of exchange and barter, and are considered more especially valuable as enabling the happy possessor to indulge in a proportionable increase in the number of his wives—twenty oxen being the usual equivalent for a wife sound in wind and limb and free from blemish. The wives agree well together, each living in her separate hut, so that a large establishment is like a colony of beehives, and keeps throwing out offshoots on every fresh addition to the harem. These circular huts are generally situated on the side of a hill for shelter from wind and storm, and always harmonize well with their surroundings.

The Zulus make a kind of beer called *outchualla*, which is strong and not unpalatable. This is prepared by the women, who make quite a secret of the process. I do not know the ingredients. Like the Hottentots the Zulus turn the ant-heaps, which are as numerous here as elsewhere, to account, by making a fire with sticks at the side of the heap near the ground in a hole, which they scrape out of the hard earth. The heap soon becomes almost red-hot, then, shaving off the top, they place the animal or bird to be cooked on the flat surface, covering it over with loose earth. In a very short time the cooking is completed. Birds are first plunged into scalding water, which causes the feathers and skin to come off easily. I have seen on the frontier a large ant-heap converted into a series of ovens by scraping out holes at different points at the sides; the ant-heap is then heated in the usual way, and four or five dishes are kept going at the same time. The earth of which these ant-heaps are composed is strongly impregnated with formic acid by the ants, and this has the effect of turning it into a hard substance, almost like firebrick, in which state it easily acquires heat on the application of fire, and retains it for a considerable time, the whole surface glowing like a lime-kiln, and forming a splendid extempore cooking-range with small expenditure of fuel.

The river contains alligators and iguanas and the larger kinds of snakes. Pythons are found in abundance at Natal. The *imamba*, a small species of boa, is the most dangerous. Puff-adders are also common.

The witch doctor is all powerful here, as elsewhere in South Africa. He has unlimited power, the lives of innocent persons often being sacrificed to his cupidity or malice. No form of religion exists. The Zulus have, strange to say, the same curious rites at the approach of maturity as the Amakosae, young men at the age of fifteen being obliged to undergo a species of purification. At this period they retire to some out of the way region in the bush, where they are covered from head to foot with a solution of white clay for so many days, and kept scrupulously apart from their fellows. I once came across one of these young men anointed in this fashion when I was riding alone in a secluded spot, and was considerably startled at his unearthly appearance. On discovering me he glided into the bush. This whitewashing process is preparatory to the rite of circumcision, after undergoing which he is considered to have attained to the rank of manhood, is presented with an *assegai*, and ranked among the warriors. Each collection of *kraals* is subject to a chief. These chiefs again have allegiance to the king or great chief, as in Kaffir-land.

Conspicuous among the variety of birds at Natal is the Great King Eagle. This formidable creature will attack a man, striking with his powerful wings, and is with difficulty disabled. Besides these, ostriches, secretary birds, innumerable varieties of storks, bustards, and wild ducks, throng the rivers and *veldt* in this fine game country.

It now only remains to notice the Dutch colonists. The part most thickly populated by them is the territory of the Transvaal, so lately taken over by the British Government, and which was the seat of the Dutch Republic, formed by a colony of Boers, who, migrating from the Cape, formed themselves into an independent state, which it seems, were it not for our interference, would, in all probability, by this time, have passed out of their hands into the possession of the native tribes surrounding it.

The Transvaal is a large tract of country, affording pasturage for innumerable herds of cattle, and would be well adapted for farming were it not for the disastrous droughts, to which the whole country is subject. As it is, beyond the fine oat crops, which supply food for the hardy Cape horses, and an occasional field of Indian corn, a very insignificant portion of it is devoted to arable purposes. The Dutch Boers, who inhabit it, are an uncouth race, living a patriarchal life in the midst of their flocks, and seldom making their appearance in the settlements beyond an occasional visit for the purpose of replenishing their stores, or bringing in their stock or produce for sale. They are tall as a rule, but sallow, hard-featured, indolent, and phlegmatic. They live very simply, their diet consisting of kid flesh and milk, with quantities of coffee, which they drink at all times and seasons. They are excellent shots, and make nothing of bowling over a gnu or spring-buck at three hundred yards with their long *roers*, or smooth bore guns.

Further away still, occupying isolated spots in the wide game-frequented *veldt*, live a race of Dutchmen, who eke out a miserable existence upon the game, whence they have acquired the name of Wildebeest Boers; antelope flesh, with the addition of a little meal, forming the main part of their subsistence. They rear large herds of goats, and tend small herds of large headed *trek* oxen, living in miserable mud huts, men, women, and children herding indiscriminately together. Every now and then their scanty crops are swept off by swarms of locusts, which quickly make an end of every green thing on their farms. When this happens they are obliged to pack up their household goods and *trek* away bodily with their flocks to some distant part of the *veldt*, where they can find grass and water. Following in the train of these pests two kinds of locust birds make their appearance, and certainly do their best to diminish the numbers.

The Greater Locust-Eater is a large bird of the crane tribe, with white plumage and powerful beak, which, with the legs, is of a bright red colour. The smaller species resemble, though on a larger scale, the common swallow; but have a most singular flight, wheeling swiftly about in the air, and performing the most intricate evolutions, now advancing in the shape of a wedge, with the point foremost, *anon* sweeping into a perfect crescent, then again rapidly changing front and coming on in a compact *phalanx*. These changes are so sudden that the eye can hardly follow, and seem to be made out of the pure wantonness of frolicsome enjoyment.

These, however, are not the only enemies the locusts have to fear. I have seen horses, dogs, and fowls eat them greedily. But so stupendous are the swarms, that they have been known to cross rapid rivers driven by the wind (upon which they are very dependent) dry shod upon the backs of the myriads of their fellow pioneers who have fallen into the stream in their advance, and so bridged it over with their dead bodies. To imagine walking over heaps of boiled shrimps which crackle and slip away from under the feet as one treads, will give a very good idea of their appearance and colour; and to realize that every tree and bush is heaped up with them in such a way as to leave no sign of a leaf visible, would afford some notion of their powers of destruction. When riding through a swarm, it gives the impression of looking through lattice-work, and they are carried with such force by the wind that one gets regularly pelted and sometimes well-nigh blinded by the hard raps which they inflict in their headlong flight.

Apropos of locusts, I was riding one day in the colony, in company with Colonel S., to whose eccentricities I have before alluded, on a tour of inspection, when, on our way to Fort Beaufort, we encountered a veritable swarm of locusts, by which we were enveloped on all sides—a perfect hailstorm of insects. All at once, I was startled by an exclamation, and, turning round, observed the little colonel put his hand to his eye, which was evidently smarting violently from the effect of a blow administered by one of these blundering insects.

"I'll serve you out for that, you little beast," ejaculated Colonel S. with a volley of expletives, and, turning round to his orderly, he demanded if he happened to have such a thing as a pin about him. The orderly grinned, and, after much ineffectual searching, at last produced the pin and presented it with a salute to the colonel, who, seizing the offending insect, which he had adroitly captured, between his finger and thumb, at once proceeded to transfix it, hissing out between his teeth as he gave the pin a vicious twirl, "You'll hit me in the eye, will you, will you?" (another twirl.) The locust was then put carefully back into one of his saddle holsters. It was but a brief respite however; for, will it be believed, every extra twinge of pain in the injured optic was the signal for the withdrawal of the culprit from the holster, and its subjection to fresh torments at the hands of its remorseless captor.

The Transvaal territory has now become our property, and is so far valuable as containing the diamond fields, but otherwise of little account for the value of its imports or for the purpose of colonization, and has only been the means of adding another responsibility to our much too widely extended possessions.

CHAPTER 9

The Diamond Fields

I shall give a slight sketch of the diamond fields, which I should not be satisfied altogether to pass over as the only element of importance in our new possessions in Griqua land. This tract of country was ceded to us by the Griqua chief, Adam Kock, in 1871, and is divided into the three magistracies of Pniel, Klip Drift, and Griqua town. So much information has been already afforded on this subject in Mr. Boyle's interesting work, *To the Cape for Diamonds*, that my notice of it will be very cursory indeed.

All diggings, gold or otherwise, have much in common—they attract all classes of people, of whom the rowdy element is generally conspicuous, and the diamond diggings of Griqua land may compare well in this respect with most other fields, the gentleman element rather predominating. Social distinction is no particular advantage, however; the strong arm, the resolute will, the good constitution, and the capacity for sustained labour—these are the elements of success. And yet, with all these, luck, if there be such an element, must always apparently enter into combination, as without it even pluck and labour seem unavailing. Nothing is more common, for example, than the finding of a gem of value either lying on the loose open soil, or perhaps kicked inadvertently out of a chance lump of earth, which may be the means of bestowing a small fortune upon the lucky finder. On the other hand, the most unremitting toil in a purchased claim, on a soil where every condition favourable to the discovery of diamonds seems present, may be utterly unavailing, or at least, after months of toil, yield so unremuneratively that it will not pay the working expenses. Chance, with its curious inconsistency, rules here as powerfully as elsewhere.

The diamond fields lie distant some seven or eight hundred miles from Cape Town; the favourite route being by Port Elizabeth, from which place Messrs. Cobbe's American transport carts make the distance (between four and five hundred miles) in five and a half days, for which the fare is about £12, leaving a difference of £3 for sea route from the Cape. By this route also comes all the trade with the fields. The river-diggings of Pniel and Klip Drift were, I believe, the first exploited to any extent for diamonds, the government fixing upon the latter as their headquarters. But these unimportant villages soon gave way to the more promising dry-diggings at Dutoitspan, New Rush, and Debeers, and were, after a time, comparatively deserted.

Diamonds were first found on the surface soil, the diggings seldom exceeding three to five feet in depth, the idea being that it was of no use going farther down. This, however, was soon discovered to be an erroneous theory, the grey pebbly earth lying beneath called *tufaceous* limestone, proving much richer in yield than the surface soil; the diamondiferous earth being found in layers alternately with bands of unproductive strata down to great depths, and shafts after a time of fifty feet and over were frequently sunk and found productive until the bed rock was reached; in fact, there is, I believe, no practical limit to its productiveness.

Mr. Dunn, in his clever pamphlet on the diamond fields, gives the following analysis. Firstly, with regard to the siftings of the surface sand.

These consist of a few small nodules of carbonate of lime, diamonds (from microscopic ones to ten carats in weight), small water-worn agates, chalcedony exactly like the Vaal River stones, but seldom reaching the size of a bean;

small but angular and sometimes rounded fragments of red spinel, black ditto, garnet, a green transparent mineral (*peridot*), a transparent colourless mineral resembling topaz, a few small quartz crystals, calcspar, small fragments of hematite, ostrich egg, shell fragments, bits of bone, arrow heads, and stone drippings; but the bulk of the sortings is composed of broken fragments of shell, sandstone, etc. The refuse which passes through the sieve is principally reddish-brown *silicious* sand (largely composed of crystals), with a percentage of minute fragments of red and black spinel, transparent green mineral *titaniferous* iron, and sandstone. If properly cleaned, the sortings constitute about one-tenth of the surface soil.

Secondly, as regards the *tufaceous* limestone which frequently succeeds the surfacing, he finds that:

The sortings principally consist of small lime nodules and concretions, with bits of shell occasionally. On breaking the small concretionary nodules, a nucleus is generally disclosed, consisting of one or the other of the above minerals. Sometimes it is a diamond; and though diamonds are probably as numerous in the *calcareous* layers as in the surface covering of sand, fewer are found, doubtless owing to their coating of lime. This might be remedied by the use of water or a careful pounding. When dried, the fine particles which pass through the sieve consist of grains of sand and carbonate of lime, nearly one half of the *calcareous* stuff has to be sorted as it is generally damp; and during the process of sifting, instead of passing through, forms into pills, arrow heads, eggshells, and the same materials as occur in the surfacing, are sparingly distributed.

The bed rock (of decomposed *igneous* formation), into which the lime layer gradually shades, is for the first two or three feet dry and crumbling, lumps of sand cemented by carbonate of lime, under-composed fragments of *igneous* rock, and fragments sometimes rounded of *mica, schist, gneiss* and shale. The sortings are mostly composed of *steatitic* clay, that appears firm when dry, but when wet falls into powder, bronze coloured *mica* in lumps and scales, small coarse pieces of spinel *pleonaste*.

The country surrounding the dry-diggings is even more bare and desolate looking than usual. The vast plains are covered with the everlasting *karoo* bush and the most scanty herbage. Isolated farms are scattered here and there, occupied by detached families of Boers of the usual *veldt* class, dirty, lethargic, and uncouth, and supply food for sheep which seem to thrive on the scanty pasture; but the plains are dreary, monotonous, and stony, cracked here and there with deep *sloots* or *nullahs*, formed by the tropical rains, overflowing at times with water, but never dammed up or turned to any useful account.

There is nothing very new to say about the diggings. These huge encampments, with their busy thousands, are arranged in streets and lanes of wood and canvas, each having its square, and its rude hotels, and stores overflowing with goods heaped up within and without; the wooden houses of the better class being imported ready made from the colony. These mushroom towns are surrounded on all sides by the usual intricate network of diggings, each claim allotted being limited to thirty square feet, and the ground honeycombed to such an extent by the workings, that it is a matter of difficulty to find a way between them; the adjoining claims are excavated so rigorously that the earthy partitions, at last reduced to nil, are constantly giving way and imperilling the lives of the diggers.

The *modus operandi* employed by the dry diggers, is thus described by Mr. Boyle:

The dry gritty soil of the *tufaceous* limestone is crushed into cakes of all sizes, from that of a walnut downwards; when adhering in a large mass it often has sufficient elasticity to resist considerable pounding, and such rebellious lumps are thrown aside and used for the building of walls and such like purposes; the smaller pieces and those broken up with ease are loaded in carts, piled in sacks or buckets, and conveyed by some means to the sieve. They are first passed through an instrument of coarse mesh which throws out the larger lumps. For the fine sieve, the form of a parallelogram is most used in the fields. It is about three feet long by eighteen inches broad, with a stout wooden frame and a bottom of perforated zinc or iron wire. At one end are two handles made by elongating the sides of the frame. The sifter fixes in the ground two posts; to these he suspends the ends of his sieve by a rope at each corner. Grasping the handles to hold it horizontally, he directs the Kaffir labourer to pile up a heap of stuff. He then, with an easy and untiring motion, works it about upon the sieve backwards and forwards. The nodules grind against each other and mostly break. The finer parts fly off in a cloud of villainous dust, or drop beneath through the meshes of the wire. When nothing is left but the little dry lumps like fine gravel and the diamonds, he unhooks the sieve and carries the contents to a neighbouring table, on which it is poured before the sifter. The sifter's table is about three feet by two feet six inches, perfectly smooth and fitted with a rim round three sides. He is armed with an iron scraper with which he helps himself to a convenient quantity of the stuff and spreads it out before him, picks out the stones (if any), and finally turns the refuse off the board, these acts being performed by three quick motions.

With regard to the river-diggings, the operation consists in excavating the boulders and pebbles. The boulders are piled up, but the pebbles are put through a coarse sieve or grating. Everything over two-thirds of an inch in diameter is thrown aside as refuse (any diamond of this size would catch the eye); the finer portion is either taken by cart, barrow, or bucket to the edge of the river, and washed in a cradle—a machine, the simplest form of which is a box with rockers underneath. On the top of it, and fitting one into the other, are two and sometimes three sieves or hoppers, with different meshes; the finest, having eight holes to the inch, being placed at the bottom. These hoppers are made of perforated zinc or wire, the latter being preferable. The gravel to be washed is put into the top sieve, water poured on, and the cradle worked backward and forward by a long handle, standing up vertically from the back of it. The water passes through the different sieves, taking with it all the particles smaller than the very fine mesh at the bottom. When sufficiently washed, the stuff remaining in the different sieves is placed upon a table, at which the sorter is seated.

With river-drift it is usual to sort in the shade, as so many wet bright stones are apt to dazzle the eyes. In sorting, a piece of thin sheet-iron or a knife is used. A small quantity of washed drift is scattered by the scraper over the board, and then scraped off; or the residue from the coarse sieve is placed in a cylinder, covered with wire or perforated zinc (about eight holes to the inch). By means of a simple contrivance, a part of the cylinder opens and closes tightly. Through the ends of the cylinder an axle is inserted, with a handle at one end. The cylinder is placed with the ends of the axle on opposite sides of the tub containing water; gravel is then put in, the handle turned, and all fine material and sand worked through the perforations. After a few turns in the first tub, it is placed in a second, containing cleaner water, and with a few turns more is ready for the sorting table. By this latter plan a little water can be made to serve for a long time, and it saves the labour of carrying the diamond drift to the river.

These river-diggings at Gong-Gong, on the Orange River and elsewhere, though not yielding to such a large extent as the dry, yet offer a fair remuneration, and the stones, if not so numerous, are of good quality; whilst the chances of hitting upon a first-rate gem are almost equally good; in which case the lucky finder may realise a fortune. Then, again, the scenery is very varied and land fertile, especially on the banks of the Orange River, which is a really noble stream of clear water running rapidly, and is passed by means of *ponts*, but otherwise unnavigated, having an average width of half a mile. This stream is not very deep in ordinary times—seldom exceeding three or four feet, and in summer quite fordable in most parts; but when flooded, it attains a depth of thirty to forty feet, when it becomes a formidable torrent; and at such times its banks on either side may be seen crowded with ox wagons and cattle waiting for its subsidence.

Some of the pebbles and agates which are found in its bed are very handsome. I have picked up a kind of green jade or *chalcedony*, which is beautifully mottled, and is so soft that it can be cut with a knife, and can be formed into bowls for pipes with very good effect. When passing the Orange River, on my way into the colony, I purchased a curious pipe, fashioned of this stone by an ingenious young Boer, who had not only carved the bowl very cleverly with an ordinary penknife, but had improvised a lathe and turned a brass top or lid to it very neatly; the stem being formed of gnu horn. The surrounding soil being very friable, is scraped away by the stream on both sides, so that the river runs in a kind of trench, or cutting, which is the case with many of the African rivers.

When the expedition under the command of General Sir G. Cathcart halted here on its way to Plaatberg (Moshesh's country) the Orange River was up, and running liquid mud at a fearful rate; and as there was only one *pont* available, it was proposed that the cavalry should swim their horses over. A young lancer officer was heard to remark, as he pulled vexatiously at an incipient moustache, "Oh, I say, come old fellow, I am not going to let £3,000 a year float down that (adjective) stream."

However, whilst they were talking it over, Captain Bramly of the Cape Mounted Rifles cut the Gordian-knot, taking off the bank into the stream; and having made good his passage, the rest followed, fortunately without accident, as the horses were soon out of their depth and had to swim for it.

Matters went well at the fields, and the yield of diamonds instead of diminishing seeming to increase, claims in the frontier diggings began to reach incredible prices. At New Rush, for example, (one of the best of the dry-diggings) a claim of thirty feet by seven inches fetched the enormous amount of £1,500, and none but the very rich could afford to buy more than a half or a quarter claim. When the fields were in full vigour the monthly yield of diamonds was estimated by the government at £300,000; the total report not falling far short of £3,000,000 for the current year.

Diamonds are at best but an article of luxury, and the attempt to force them in such quantities upon the market already supplied from Brazil and Golconda was disastrous, and the consequence of this enormous supply flowing into the market ended, as might naturally be expected, in a panic. In 1872, diamonds fell 10 per cent, at a leap, and the market has never entirely recovered from this depression. The consequence is that the poorer class of diggers is driven out of the fields, and, as is now the case in Australia and elsewhere, the fields are worked by means of companies and rich speculators, who can afford to wait their time to realize.

With regard to the quality of the diamonds, Mr. Boyle, who has studied the subject, describes the Cape diamond as differing from the Brazilian and Indian in several respects. The coat or skin which is invariably found enveloping the latter being quite wanting in the Cape gem, which from its high polish, and the absence of this *pellicle*, is as bright and clear as glass, more accurate and symmetrical also in its angles, which are sharp and clearly defined, and sometimes even fluted. Many tinted stones are found, from the faintest tinge of yellow, green or bluish and but rarely rose, to the full coloured positive shades of orange, blue, green, and oven brown (called fancy stones) and fetching a fancy price accordingly.

Another peculiarity of the Cape diamonds is, that they are apt to crack and split in a very extraordinary manner, sometimes within a few hours of their being taken out of the ground, sometimes after an interval of months. Parcels of stones which have been sent home by the mail consigned to the mercantile houses in England and numbered carefully have shown in the invoice returned a greater number of stones than described; which curious discrepancy is to be explained by the fact of one or more of the stones having exploded into fragments in transition; in which case their value would be enormously depreciated.

It is curious and amusing to remark the effect produced by the discovery of the diamond fields upon the Boer population of the Transvaal and Free State; of those, that is, whose farms lay within or adjoining the area opened up by these discoveries. As they watched the routes to the different encampments, and saw the whole adjoining country thronged with people of all classes flocking to the different centres, they were simply stupefied with amazement, and were quite helpless. They did make a feeble attempt to withstand the tide of emigration, as far as lay in their power, by placing what obstacles they could in the way, as they saw their farms overrun; but it was of no avail, and before long, being naturally greedy of gain and saving almost to penuriousness in their habits, they gradually yielded to the all-powerful influence of their surroundings, and *trekked* off one by one to try their fortunes with the rest.

They soon found that they had great advantages over their brother diggers. They had always their farms to fall back upon for supplies, which, being raised at home, cost them comparatively little. They would start off themselves with their wagons, and at the same time leave their farms in charge of their families, which, being proverbially large, supplied sufficient hands to carry on the necessary farm operations, so that they suffered little loss on this account. Then, again, the Boer is an indolent, apathetic being, who may be said to exist rather than to live, and whose ambition is to be let alone and enjoy his ease amongst his flocks and herds, seldom moving beyond his farm, unless to make periodical visits, accompanied by his numerous progeny, to his *kirk*—for they are great churchgoers. Time thus being no object to him, he could well afford to bide until some run of luck should reward his toil.

Again, the stranger to the soil was put to a constant expense for food and shelter, paying dearly for the scanty accommodation he enjoyed, and always more or less dependent upon the weather for his comfort. The latter was liable to be soaked out of his tent when it rained, or perhaps almost washed away by the tropical torrent—unless he was an old campaigner and understood how his tent should be secured—or blown down bodily when exposed to the fierce winds which sometimes swept over the unsheltered flats. This very catastrophe occurred in my own case, when we were encamped at Plaatberg; the force of the gale being so great, that it blew my bell-tent flat (notwithstanding that the pegs were extra long and were bushed underneath), and scattered my papers in such a manner that I had to chase some of them half a mile over the plain before I could secure them.

The Boer's wagon, on the other hand, was his castle. Here he lived, slept, and took his meals; protected from sun and rain by the substantial canvas tilt which covered his abode; whilst his oxen grazed on the *veldt*. Here he remained patiently toiling and content, shifting his ground as often as he pleased, and replenishing his supplies when exhausted. When he had realised a handsome sum by his exertions, he would spend his newly-acquired riches in making large additions to his flocks and herds, which he could turn to good account by selling again to the camps in the shape of meat or transport; so that he made money all ways.

They may perhaps be classed amongst the few diggers who can be said to have derived substantial benefit from their labours; as they spent next to nothing, and never gambled, and added little support to the canteen-keeper, who was the chief drain upon the pocket of the diamond seeker; nor is the Boer sufficiently excitable to be permanently affected in his habits by the feverish influence of the race for wealth. For the latter, I take it, is one of the most objectionable phases of the digger's trade; that it incapacitates him for any steady pursuit, and makes him reckless and improvident, and in its moral deterioration affects him most injuriously in his after life; a prospect poorly compensated for indeed by the trifling amount of worldly benefit secured to him by his gains, which he mostly dissipates on the scene of his exploits.

Chapter 10

Graaf Reinet

One of the thoroughly Dutch towns I visited was Graaf Reinet, which is situated some six hundred miles from Graham's Town, and preserves its Dutch characteristics beyond most others, being seldom visited by English traders.

My mission there was to fetch three deserters from my regiment, of whose capture we had received tidings. To accomplish this object I was sent from headquarters with an escort of twelve mounted men. Our road lay through rather an uninteresting country; consisting principally of a vast plain covered with *karoo* bush, varied occasionally by wild rocky passes or *kloofs*, full of baboons. These stony *kloofs* afforded shelter to innumerable *dassics*, or rock rabbits; singular little creatures between a rat and a rabbit, of a dark-brown colour, destitute of tail, whose feet, denuded of fur, and covered with black leather cuticle, proclaim it as belonging to the order of *pachydermata*. These we often observed peeping from their holes or standing upright upon their hind legs, intently listening with a curiously inquisitive air, popping suddenly back into their hiding-place when they caught sight of our party.

This stony desolate country is one of the favourite haunts of the porcupine, little heaps of whose quills we found amongst the bushes; the frequency of them proving how easily they are detached from the skin. The fable of the porcupine shooting out its quills, is thus easily explained. When molested and unable to escape, it makes sudden rushes, always in a backward direction, piercing its enemy with its quills, which then become detached and remain sticking where they enter, often inflicting severe wounds. It has of course no power to project them. One which I shot, as it was running along the banks of a small river, proved on examination to be perfectly infested with enormous fleas. The frequent existence of parasites, instances of which I also observed amongst the large game of the plains, and which appears to be common to all living organisms, is a curious fact.

> Great fleas have little fleas
> Upon their legs to bite 'em,
> These again have smaller fleas,
> And so ad infinitum—

as Swift hath it!

On our route we had a singular encounter with a bushman; singular, because these strange little beings are rarely seen in the Colony; living as they do in the interior, being averse to civilisation; and, above all things, detesting anything like regular employment. Like the Ishmaelites of old, every man's hand is against them; the Boers in the interior actually hunting them down like wild animals. They are indeed the pariahs of the plains, and have never been known to mix with other tribes. Nor does their language (if such it can be called) resemble that of any other race with whom we have come in contact, The Amakosae, however, seem, strange to say, to have partially adopted their peculiar click in their own high-sounding language; which is almost as sonorous as the Greek, and consisting principally of vowels, is admirably adapted for conveying sound, and it is no unusual thing to hear them conversing together from the tops of the lofty detached hills, which they appear to do with ease at incredible distances with most musical effect. The bushmen are completely isolated as a people, and are indeed more fit to herd with animals than with human beings.

This strange little creature had made his resting place near a little *vley*, or pool of brackish water, where we had halted one hot day, nothing better being available, and eyed us with evident fear and suspicion. I gathered from one of the Hottentots, who seemed to understand his mysterious jargon, that he had taken service on some Boer's farm in the Colony, and was returning to his native wilds for the purpose of enjoying once more his lost freedom.

He seemed to have accumulated some earthly possessions during his sojourn, being heavily laden with all kinds of odds and ends. He was clad in an old suit of somebody else's clothes, which being quite contrary to his habits, was of itself sufficiently extraordinary, and was possessed of a long Dutch *roer*, and four or five bags or sacks made of skins, which were full of some kind of plunder, and he had actually adopted the wild cat skin pouch with its gay worsted tassels, so dear to the colonial Hottentot. Seizing the opportunity, I took out my notebook, and was about to put him down on paper. My little friend regarded my doings, however, with great uneasiness, looking upon it, as the Hottentots afterwards explained to me, as a species of enchantment which would give me some kind of power over him, a feeling in which, I observed, the superstitious Hottentots evidently shared. So without more ado he packed up his traps in a hurried manner, slinging everything, bags, sacks, etc., by their leather thongs, around him, and before I could achieve even an outline, marched off, his long *roer* projecting on either side of his shoulders, saltire-wise, in most ludicrous fashion, the weapon being actually larger than himself, and was off in *a jiffy* in spite of all my entreaties backed up by offers of money, which were powerless to detain him.

I found Graaf Reinet primitive but positively charming after the arid country through which we had approached it. The streets were lined on both sides with Kaffir *boems* and acacia trees in full flower. Running streams of clear water ran in paved channels by the pathways, and the one-storied houses, each furnished with a *stoep* or raised platform of stone in front, were dazzling white, contrasted as they were with their green doors and window-shutters. The windows, extending in some houses over the entire face of the building, were constructed of innumerable little panes of glass, which gave them a very bizarre effect.

The Kaffir *boem*, with which the streets are adorned, is a very beautiful tree. The flower, which is bright scarlet, almost dazzles one's eyes to look at, and resembles in form our scarlet-runner, but is infinitely larger, and, being provided with long hanging stamens, has a very imposing appearance. The tree grows to a considerable size, and branches out handsomely, the flower showing before the leaf, but is seen in its greatest perfection when the brilliant blossoms are framed in its rich canopy of tropical foliage, at which time it presents a splendid object in the landscape.

We succeeded, with the help of the authorities, in not only capturing our three deserters, but carried back with us a man belonging to the 91st Foot, who had deserted seven years before from the headquarters of his regiment. He was a fine sunburnt looking man about thirty, who, tired of the quiet uneventful life he had been leading in the *veldt*, had actually given himself up rather than remain any longer away from his brethren. I felt quite a pity for him, as he seemed a very decent fellow, and I might have got myself into a very pretty scrape on his account, had he been less trustworthy.

It happened in this wise. He had so gained my confidence on the way home, that on his earnestly requesting permission to visit a Dutch Boer who lived on a farm near the spot where we had made our camp in whose hands he had left a certain sum due to him as wages, I actually allowed him to go unaccompanied (at his particular request) by an escort, he promising to return the same evening. I had no sooner done so, than I began to repent my folly; and as he did not make his appearance that evening, the unenviable state of mind in which I passed the night may be imagined, my disturbed dreams teeming with courts-martial and all kinds of horrors. Judge of my relief, however, when on the next morning my friend came sauntering leisurely into the camp, and reported himself in the most matter-of-fact manner. I need hardly say that I was an inexperienced sub. in those days, and I well remember the grin on my sergeant's face, when I hinted to him in course of conversation that morning that "perhaps it would be as well not to mention anything about this little episode at headquarters."

WILD DOGS HUNTING ZEBRA

In a country so favourable to escape there were, as may be imagined, many deserters wandering about the Colony, supplied from that numerous class so common to our armies, the *mauvais sujets,* and they were often discovered in out-of-the-way spots by the colonists themselves, upon the principle of *set a thief to catch a thief*, many of these settlers having been old soldiers, who had taken farms or set up wayside inns for the refreshment of travellers.

One knowing old fellow, who kept an inn of this sort on the main road, had gained quite a notoriety for his success in this respect, which he invariably achieved by the following expedient. When one of these suspicious gentry entered his homestead, the settler's antecedents soon enabled him, from old habit, to detect some little peculiarity of bearing or gesture which was sufficient to stamp the wanderer. Then quietly waiting his opportunity, and approaching his man from behind, he would suddenly call out in stentorian tones "Attention!" Springing up at the familiar word of command, to the accustomed attitude, down would go the arms on either side, the little fingers posed on a line with the seams of the overalls with mathematical precision (*vide* drill book), and our friend was trapped and could only surrender at discretion.

I found the Dutch Boers, who lived on the isolated farms, which we generally contrived to make our halting-places at night, very hospitable. On approaching a house I usually rode up and requested permission to *outspan*, and when the phlegmatic Dutchman, after a prolonged stare out of his lacklustre eyes, had got over his astonishment at my appearance, his long-drawn *"Yaah, mynheer, as ye woll,"* was a signal for our dismounting and making preparation for the night's bivouac. The men would place their heavy cavalry saddles in a row in front of the horses. They unstrapped their cloaks and, if there was no shelter, slept wrapped up in them on their saddle-blankets; the horses were linked together by their head-stalls behind the saddles, under a horse-guard. The deserters were handcuffed to the men, and I found quarters for myself inside with *mynheer*.

I could talk very little Dutch at this time, so that I found it, at first, rather awkward. The primitive dinner generally commenced with my host's ejaculation, *"Kom sitt,"* upon which invitation I took my place at the table. The meal usually consisted of kid-flesh, roasted or boiled, with rice and raisins, little *commitjies*, or bowls of milk, being placed by the side of each person in the absence of liquor. They had a kind of *maag* bitter, which they drank. before dinner, by way of an appetiser, and was the only kind of fermented drink I ever saw in their houses, with the exception of a coarse kind of spirit, termed *Bucca brandy*, made, I believe, from the seeds of a bush of that name, growing in the *veldt*. The most disagreeable part of the entertainment was the swarm of flies, which flocked from all quarters when we were at table; the Dutchmen's cattle *kraals*, or thorny enclosures made to keep the herds from straying at night, being always placed in close proximity to their front doors was the cause of our being almost eaten up by them.

The *kraal* fly is a small, exceedingly pertinacious insect, only to be driven away or dislodged after repeated efforts, and darts his proboscis into your flesh, always leaving his irritating little sting behind. They covered the meat, and committed suicide in the milk by hundreds, and were indeed a perfect pest. In the better kind of farm-houses a Hottentot girl is generally employed at meal-time to brush them away with a *chowrie*.

The beds were huge square platforms of heavy wood planted on four legs, and the clothing consisted of a huge feather mattress, not always of the sweetest kind, and a *veldt comberse*, or quilt, made of a blanket sewn up in a sheet of cotton print, and, apparently, never washed. Payment was, in most cases, absolutely declined by the hospitable host, although liberal rations of oat hay were invariably supplied to our troopers.

A three weeks' march brought us back to Graham's Town none the worse for our trip. I was glad to hear that my protégé, the deserter, was treated leniently by the court martial which adjudicated upon his case; his voluntary rendering up of himself having been taken into consideration, together with his previous good character, and I have no doubt that he will yet do good service.

Chapter 11

Kaffir Warfare—its Peculiarities

Some discriminating individual has truly observed, with more originality than elegance, that a Kaffir war is "the snob of all wars." In this service the British warrior neither lives nor dies like a gentleman. Opposed to savages, who are in the habit of skulking behind stones and bushes, and literally stalking their opponents, he falls ingloriously, without seeing his enemy and deprived even of the poor satisfaction of a shot in return.

The Kaffir has a strong objection to expose himself in the open plains, preferring to remain, spiderlike, in his web, waiting till his foe shall become entangled in some position sufficiently difficult to allow him to commence his attack with every advantage in his favour. Should he find himself hard pressed, he retreats from bush to bush with marvellous dexterity, delivering his fire and then sinking, as it were, into the very earth, without offering any visible point of attack. And this, too, in ground where a hare or a partridge could alone apparently find cover. Equally unsatisfactory when killed, "he cuts up badly;" his personal property, in all likelihood, consisting of nothing more valuable than one or two brass curtain-rings, an old curb-chain, which serves him in *lieu* of a bracelet, with two or three *assegais*, very inferior in point of workmanship, and a Brummagem-looking gun, which might be purchased in any civilised country for ten shillings. His pouch, of rough un-tanned leather, will probably contain some twelve or thirteen zinc or leaden bullets, badly cast, with their jagged edges left uncut, and a small bunch of charmed twigs, with which his prophet Umlangeni has provided him, as a sure protection against sudden death; of a verity they have profited him little.

Cattle constitute his worldly wealth, and only means of traffic and exchange. Should he wish to marry, the problem stands thus: Given so many cows, find the style of wife required—her beauty and accomplishments rising in an exact ratio to the number of horns he can bring into the market. Does he commit murder, or rob his comrades, the foul disgrace is only to be wiped away with cattle; which lapse, as a sort of fine, to his chief, who is seldom debarred, by modest scruples, from taking them. To wrest these from his strongholds is the glorious aim of the British soldier; indeed the art and mystery of cattle-driving, as practised at Smithfield, may be considered indispensable should he wish to be famous in Kaffir warfare; the successful warrior being estimated less by the number of scalps which adorn his belt, or the excellence of his manoeuvres in the field, than by the number of heifers he may drive, patriarchal like, before his victorious columns.

The regular forces employed for the subjugation of these scoundrels being small, Her Majesty calls in the assistance of levies from various parts of the country. Some of these are Europeans; the remainder embrace every variety of caste, from the "Day and Martin" coloured Mozambique nigger to the parchment-faced bushman. Here may be seen runaway sailors, discharged soldiers, scamps out of employ, and ragged rascals of every description, who prefer the glorious profession of arms to hard work of any kind. Like all soldiers clothed and shod by contract, their outfit, furnished by the slop-sellers, exhibits, as might be supposed, an agreeable variety of costume,—the military forage cap mingling sociably with the *paletot* and short boots of private life. Their sense of discipline not being strict, they are accustomed to look upon the most ordinary commands of their superior officers as admitting of argument.

Thus, when required to mount sentry, they consider their doing so as a *personal favour*, and are apt, after remaining, as they suppose, a sufficiently long time upon the watch, to notify the fact to the corporal of the guard by firing off their muskets, possibly shooting some stray wanderer who is unfortunate enough to cross their beats. This is looked upon as *fortune de la guerre,* and does not discompose them. This noble indifference to human life is, perhaps, as strongly exhibited on patrol as elsewhere, one officer and four privates having been destroyed in this manner on the five first successive patrols by these worthies (their style of firing being distributed amongst friends and foes indiscriminately and impartially).

Nothing can give an adequate idea of their grotesque appearance on the line of march. The utter absence of all regularity, their guns sloping at a hundred different angles, their rolling gait, the number of miscellaneous odds and ends they carry, and loose ropes towing overboard. They are perfectly uncontrollable, their officers having abandoned all idea of discipline as hopeless. Thus they go along in a confused rabble, each one walking at his own pace, and carrying his weapon as he finds most convenient, and laughing and chattering incessantly. Nothing is more difficult than to keep this volatile warrior from straggling on the line of march. Now it is a shoe coming off, or a strap giving way, or he must stop five minutes while he takes off bundle after bundle to get at his ration biscuit—his three days' supply of which he generally finishes long before he arrives at his first encampment. Then he must stop to drink at every little pool, or *vley*, of muddy water near the road, and perhaps is missing altogether, and does not turn up for some hours, when it appears he has been attracted by some pumpkin plantation, or *mealy* (Indian corn) field, of which he brings off some forty or fifty specimens, ingeniously stowed away in various parts of his person, and not unfrequently an enormous pumpkin, or perhaps two, impaled, saltire-wise, upon his musket.

Little of the *"pomp and circumstance of glorious war"* is known in Africa. Appearances are little attended to; unless on duty no one thinks of wearing uniform, and everybody has some odd notion of dress suitable to the climate, and cares little who remarks it. In quarters, wide-awakes, or pith-hats, like overgrown mushrooms, and short monkey-jackets, prevail; the short pipe not unfrequently superseding the cigar, and waistcoats not being always considered indispensable. This state of things, it must be understood, is only applicable to the frontiers. At Cape Town, which is of course the *ne plus ultra* of civilisation, the case is different. Here we have our Rotten Row, and a fashionable hour for appearing therein, clad in purple and fine linen; no officer allowed to appear out of uniform, and regulation is strictly adhered to.

In war time a delightful freedom of discipline prevails, and one fights comfortably enough. At the commencement of the campaign the troops were all habited *en bourgeois,* the scarlet coat being considered too conspicuous in the bush, and offering much too good a mark to the enemy. The *grande armée* then contained every known variety of wide-awake and shooting-jacket. As no two of these were alike, and as the patterns to be found in slop-shops are usually of a sporting character, with a strong tendency to checks and stripes, the appearance of a regiment on parade was to an unaccustomed eye odd enough.

Picture to yourself, gentle reader, in addition to these, the regular soldiers of the line, from twelve to thirteen hundred levies of every caste, colour, country, and complexion, in the same style of rig, only ten times more worn and ragged, and arm them with long Brummagem single-barrelled guns, add to these a hundred Fingo warriors, their only clothing a blanket and a woollen night cap, striped with gaudy colours, driving before them some twenty or thirty large-headed, long-legged, lean, slaughter cattle: heat up, as they say in the cookery books, with a warm African sun, and you will have an excellent recipe for the composition of a patrol about to start from any frontier town for the purpose of annihilating Kaffirs. Again, imagine these same warriors, their faces begrimed with red dust so as to be hardly recognisable by their dearest friends, with beards of fourteen days' growth, tattered clothes, and lips blackened with powder (from biting cartridges), no two walking in step, many without shoes, and dreadfully groggy on their legs, and some *dead foundered*, and you will have another pretty correct idea of the appearance of the same patrol on its return to headquarters.

Should it bring captive in its train one or two hundred head of lean cattle, it will be considered entirely successful, and the war will be looked upon as progressing favourably. Feeble-minded individuals who form their notions of war from paintings, and who vainly imagine that a soldier puts on his best clothes to fight in, would be rather surprised to see a colonel in action, leading his regiment on to glory, in the shape of a middle-aged gentleman wearing spectacles, and habited in a leathern hunting-cap, a short mackintosh, drab trousers and brass spurs, riding on a fifteen pound hack, and carrying no more formidable weapon *"to fright the souls of fearful adversaries"* than a Dollond's telescope.

Yet such things are not uncommon in Kaffir warfare; nor is the drill-book, with its intricate manoeuvres, much in requisition. It is all skirmishing. Not the skirmishing as laid down in page so-and-so of Her Majesty's Regulations, and so too frequently practised by Her Majesty's troops at present fighting in Kaffir-land; not the steady advance of a division in formal row, like backgammon men on a board, with shoulders well kept back, bodies mathematically perpendicular, and eyes elevated heavenward, firing by word of command at nothing in particular: but every man looking out for himself, and anxious to expose as little of his body as possible.

Look at the wily Kaffir, and take a lesson. Observe him as he creeps noiselessly on, anxiously making for the shelter of some friendly ant-heap or trifling irregularity in the ground, instantaneously dropping when your musket is pointed at him, and leaving no surface exposed to view. How adroitly he springs up when your bullet has whizzed harmlessly over his head, and with what deliberation he takes aim in return. Then again, how cunningly he strives to gain that little strip of bush on the flank unobserved, and seems almost to sink into the earth when you discover him. On the other hand, regard the unfortunate pipe clay bearing his great coat and field blanket, as Christian in *The Pilgrim's Progress* did his sins, in an intolerable burthen, on his shoulders, steadfastly walking after the same Kaffir in the open plain, marching along bolt upright, as if on parade; giving his wily foe five shots for his one, and disdaining concealment: and you will at once appreciate the respective merits of theory and practice.

I shall not enter into a lengthened account of the Kaffir war or the causes which preceded it, for these are already matters of history; but will give some general notions of a patrol setting out from headquarters, reprinted from a slight sketch written whilst the war of 1851 was in progress, and will add at more length some particular instances of campaigning adventures, completing my personal experience of Kaffir warfare.

CHAPTER 12

Kaffir Warfare—the Patrol

"Simpson! have you got all my traps ready for patrol?"

"Yes, sir!"

"Well, what have you got?"

"Whoy, sir," says Simpson, scratching his head to assist his memory, "there's half a 'am, a couple of cold chickens, 'cos, you ain't a-going to live on them tough rashuns as is taken hot from the cow" (cunning dog, he will have no objection to eating them himself, you will find), "a bottle of pickles, two white loaves, a corkscrew, some raspberry jam, a pair of trousers (in case them you got on gets wet), two bottles of brandy, two tin plates (which you are always a-losing), an iron fork, knife and spoon, in a case (as I gave ninepence for), a pair of hammunition boots (I calls it robbing the soldier, a gentleman a-wearing them kind of things!), a tongue," aside: "though, Heaven knows, you've got a tongue of your own,—three shirts, some pepper in a bottle (them bottles always breaks), a bag of coffee, a 'air-brush, and a bar of yellow soap: them things goes in your saddle bags. Then there's a small kittle, three blankets, a gridiron (what you ever come out to this country for, I can't think), the patrol-tent, a hoil-cloth, and a tin pot as goes on the top of the pack saddle."

"What! will old Blunderbuss carry all that?"

"Lor bless you, sir," says Simpson, "Major Buffins of the 'Land-seers,' always takes a feather bed and two dozen of sherry!"

This was the style of dialogue often carried on between myself and servant, on the eve of a fourteen days' patrol; and this is the sort of miscellaneous list of incongruous articles my unfortunate packhorse was loaded with on these occasions.

The patrol-tent, earned with me as a part of our baggage, being, as I believe, peculiar to South African warfare, a short description of it may not be unacceptable. I will defy any man who has never bivouacked under an umbrella, or lived, Diogenes-like, in a water-butt, to imagine what it is to inhabit a patrol-tent.

It is a most unaccommodating edifice. A man must reduce himself to a quadruped, and go upon *all fours* before he can get into it. He comes out in an equally ignominious manner, heels first. When he is in it for good, his life may be considered precarious. Every now and then some incautious straggler stumbles over his tent-ropes, and shakes him to his very foundation; or, it is not impossible that a loose troop-horse may gallop bodily over him, rooting him as it were out of the very earth, if nothing worse, to be set up again in the dark, with a vast deal of trouble. If it rains, he will probably pass the night with a foot of water under the small of his back, unless his servant should have been sufficiently provident to have dug a trench round his habitation. This is a mishap to which all tents are liable. The patrol-tent is, however, very portable; and, when rolled up, occupies little space, and lies easily on the top of a pack saddle.

Having got my baggage packed, we will imagine the patrol, consisting of some seven or eight hundred regulars and about a thousand levies, on its way for Kaffir-land. I am got up in the following fashion. In addition to my ordinary undress uniform I wear a light forage cap and a comfortable patrol jacket, and besides my cavalry sword I carry a double-barrelled gun, attached to the saddle in a leathern bucket on the right side, a pocket pistol loaded with French brandy is slung over my shoulders, a slice of jerked beef in *lieu* of a revolver in my holsters, and a broad strap buckled round my waist supports a good sized pouch for bullets and cartridges, and a smaller one for caps, my military cloak is rolled, on the saddle in front, and a tin pot, or *tot* in colonial parlance, adorns the horse's crupper.

None, by the bye, ever thinks of starting on any kind of expedition in South Africa without this useful appendage, which is carried to enable the thirsty traveller to drink at any of the numerous *vleys* or small rivers without prostrating himself on the soil, and dipping his nose in the limpid element. They are carried anywhere; sometimes dangling under the horse's throat, or knocking against his ribs, but oftener as described, suspended on the crupper.

"We are now fairly on the road, and have progressed two or three miles at a slow walk, when, happening to look back, I miss my packhorse. On making inquiries I find that Blunderbuss, being fresh, has kicked up his heels, and deposited my *pack* in the middle of the road, and broken a bottle of lemon syrup which was wrapped up for safety in one of my clean shirts. The pack is soon set right, and I spur on after the column, mentally consigning all packs and packhorses to perdition.

The column now enters a rugged part of the country by a winding road, flanked on either side with mimosa thorns, and has advanced a short distance, when *Whirr! Whirr! Phit! Phit!* come sundry leaden messengers from the rear, and a cry of *"Kaffirs! Kaffirs!"* steals along the column. As yet, nothing is to be seen, unless by stooping down, when a sharp and practised eye may detect a glimpse here and there of sundry copper-coloured bodies creeping along the bushes. A company of *light bobs* is sent to the rear, and extended in skirmishing order.

"Where are they? I don't see them!" I say, getting excited.

"Dar so! Darloup he! Skiet, skiet!" ("There he is! There he runs! Shoot, shoot!") exclaims a little Hottentot, who is down on one knee loading his musket.

I do not believe it; when sure enough a puff of smoke rises out of the identical bush pointed out by the far-seeing Apollo, and *ping* comes the bullet just over my head, and I struggle so hard to get my gun out of the bucket, that it goes off and blows the bottom of it out in the attempt.

The Kaffirs continue to creep up in the rear, under cover of the bushes, and a sharp fire is kept up from the column, with little effect on either side, until the road, getting more open, it ceases entirely. After a smart walk of ten miles, the column arrives at the banks of a small stream. The bugle's shrill note sounds the halt, and the army goes to breakfast.

The infantry form up and pile arms; the cavalry off saddle, and the horses are turned out, under the protection of the guard, to graze—having been previously knee-haltered. This knee-haltering is managed by taking a couple of simple half hitches round the horse's foreleg, with a strong rein, or *reim*, attached to the neck-strap, which brings his head towards the ground, effectually preventing his running away; and is indeed the common precaution taken by every South African traveller when on the road.

The men now collect wood for their fires, and make coffee. I breakfast luxuriously off a cold chicken and a tin mug of coffee made in a kettle; and top up, I am not ashamed to say, with a drop of brandy out of the case-bottle, and a short pipe; and exclaim in the fullness of my heart, or rather stomach, that "this patrolling is a jolly sort of thing, after all." After an hour's rest, the advance sounds, and the column moves on again. The Kaffirs are now seen collecting on the hills and shouting. On one tall *copjie (Anglicè* round hill) a group of mounted Kaffirs watch the course of the column, and having made their observations, suddenly scamper off, and are out of sight in a moment. These signs of the coming storm are well known, and everyone begins to get his fighting gear in readiness for a scrimmage.

The bush has been gradually getting thicker, and the road winds by a steep descent through a thickly wooded valley. Everybody knows, intuitively, that here will be the fight, and braces himself up as he nears it. The officer commanding thinks it also suspicious, and makes his dispositions accordingly. Two bodies of levies, each a hundred strong, make a wide detour on either flank; flankers are also sent out on each side of the column. The cavalry who form the advance guard, close to their centre; and those who are extended in skirmishing order in the rear, have orders to close up to the column when they approach the defile, where it is impracticable for horses, and allow the infantry to take their place.

The rear is always the principal point of attack in Kaffir warfare; the head of the column often passing unmolested through a defile full of Kaffirs, who wait until the main body has gone by, and then commence a furious onslaught upon the rear, which they will follow up pertinaciously for miles.

The fight generally commences by a tremendous fusillading on the part of the levies, who fire at least fifty shots for every one of the wily foe, and who, if not checked, will never cease firing from the first commencement, until brought up for want of ammunition. They do not fire all this ammunition at Kaffirs, but into the bush, where the foe is supposed to be; and they call this process (for, lamentable to relate, it has actually arrived at a process), *"maakin schoone de pad,"* literally translated "making clear the road;" in other words, sending their bullets where they are afraid to venture themselves.

The firing has now become general; the head of the column has passed through the defile with slight loss, and the savages are thronging in great numbers to attack the rear, when the bugle sounds the halt, and the order is given to charge back in full force upon the unsuspecting foe, who thinks, no doubt, that he will be allowed his usual privilege of hammering the rear, in which pursuit he has every advantage; when, with a tremendous shout, the redcoats come back *at the double*, and, forcing their way through the bushes, drive the frightened Amakosae flying before them. The tables are now completely turned. The Kaffirs stand not upon the order of their going, but go at once, and rush pell-mell to gain the shelter of the nearest *kloofs*. One gigantic Kaffir is limping painfully along in the vain hope of reaching cover, amidst a perfect shower of bullets, exposed to the fire of a whole company of redcoats. He is struck down repeatedly, but rises manfully each time, and at last, both legs being broken, drags himself for some yards towards the long-wished-for shelter, by clutching the grass convulsively with his hands.

It is exciting work; the troops have entered the *kloof*, and are driving the Kaffirs out of it, in parties of ten or twelve at a time, and you may be sure as they emerge from the other side that they get pretty well peppered. In the meantime, a detachment of Royal Artillery has posted two light field-pieces upon the heights, and is bowling *spherical case* into them. Everybody is yelling with excitement. It is a frightfully hot day, but the fire is so much hotter that nobody thinks of it. Everyone is firing and loading as fast as he can. I have had some twenty shots myself at Kaffirs, but I cannot exactly undertake to say that I have hit anything in particular! No wonder; for such has been my excitement, and hurry in the heat of the chase, that I have fired perhaps as often without bullets as with, and have sometimes put two cartridges into the same barrel, without being aware of it!

The pursuit has been carried through valley and over ridge; through brake and through briar, and the whole column is scattered about in every direction. It is a regular scramble, and every uniform is mixed up together. But the chase begins to slacken: the pace has been too good to last. The recall sounds; the firing dies away to a few desultory shots; and the men come straggling back in most admired disorder, puffing and blowing, with the perspiration running down at every pore. It takes a good hour to collect them.

The ground being impracticable for riding, I have left my horse, at the beginning of the fight, with one of my men, and I am returning with the *ruck* at a much slower pace than I set out. I have lost one of my spurs, my clothes are torn, and I have a pleasant smack of gunpowder in my mouth, and my lips are glued together with thirst. The column being put together, the advance sounds, and it moves on in the direction of its next encampment. The day's proceedings have been satisfactory, and the officer commanding is in a good humour. The troops have had it all their own way today; may they be equally fortunate on the morrow!

As many parts of Kaffir-land are destitute of tree or shrub; and afford no supply of firewood, the men are allowed, when approaching an encamping ground of this sort, to forage for it. on the road. Luckily, one cannot travel far in any direction, without coming across a *mealy* field or plantation of some sort surrounded by a *kraal*, or rough enclosure of thorn bushes, which supplies admirable material for this purpose. The column no sooner comes in sight of this desirable object, when "yoicks, forward!" away go blue, green, red, and brown jackets. The column, as if touched by the wand of Harlequin, dissolves in a moment, and a general scramble ensues. One walks off with a thorn bush as big as himself; another cuts down a young tree which he bears away, Atlas-like, on his shoulders; whilst some, more provident, break the wood up into small fagots, which they carry slung on their muskets. The mounted men jump off their horses, and presently come away like moving shrubberies; "Birnam Wood moving to Dunsinane," is actually verified. The whole column is a moving grove. The *kraal* melts away, and in a moment is on its way full sail to Fort White. Each man carries enough to last him through the night, and perhaps a trifle over for the benefit of his less fortunate companions, who, being employed on escort or other duty, cannot help themselves. Sometimes when the mounted men are sent on in advance of the column to save time, it is very amusing to see the disappointed equestrian, when the *trot* is sounded, dropping log after log of his vegetable hoards, or trying in vain to keep his balance at the canter, with a young tree on his shoulders.

Fort White, the scene of our next encampment, is built in the usual wattle-and-daub style of the country, and is a collection of little irregular hovels, enclosed by a mud wall, formidable against Kaffirs, but utterly indefensible against a disciplined foe. As it is only just large enough to hold its garrison, about a hundred men, the patrols encamp on the ground outside the walls. The ground has been so often used for this purpose, that it is a perfect Golgotha of ox bones, and the ground is burnt and blackened by the remains of a thousand fires. Until lately (to increase the desolation) one might detect kicking about the plain the mortal remains of sundry Kaffirs, which lay bleaching in the sun, gaunt trophies of the gallantry of the little garrison's brave resistance against a multitude of Kaffirs, who came down from the hills one morning, and attacked it in three divisions to the number of some hundreds, but were fain to retreat in confusion after a short siege, leaving some twenty or thirty of their comrades dead on the field.

As the wattle-and-daub of which the houses or hovels of Fort White are composed is the material of which half the houses in the colony are constructed, and as the reader may be inclined to ask what is wattle and what daub, it may be as well to describe it. The wattles are long rods or twigs of tough wood cut in lengths, and inserted edgeways between a framework of wood, so as to form a kind of trellis-work. The daub, is a composition of mud and cow-dung, which is plastered or daubed on to the wattles forming the walls. A roof of timber is then added, covered with reeds. The inside walls get a coating of whitewash. The floor is daubed over with the same cow-dung mixture, and the house is then considered eligible as an officer's quarter in South Africa. It is no exaggeration to say, that a civilized man in any other part of the world would hesitate before he put an ordinary hack into it.

The horses are now linked together, by fastening their reins to each other's headstalls, facing outwards—sentries are posted—tents are pitched—and I begin to think of dinner. I am dying of thirst, the case-bottle has run dry, and I am trying to extract the cork of a brandy flask with a penknife.

No one ever thinks of drinking the water at Fort White without qualifying it. It is frightfully *brack* and appears to be a combination of white clay and salt water, with a dash of *copperas* in it—so bad indeed, that tea and coffee made with it are hardly drinkable. It occasions violent diarrhoea and spasms, if drunk in any quantity. Half the small streams in Kaffir-land are *brack*. They are extremely deceptive in appearance, being as clear as crystal, and have a most inviting look to the thirsty traveller, whose face of delight, as he jumps off his horse and carries the water to his eager lips, is only to be equalled by his intense disgust, when, finding it dreadfully disagreeable, he sputters it out again.

One of my fellow cornets, confident in his resources, asks me to dine with him, and is nearly falling a victim to his rashness. He has long indulged a desire to try some tins of preserved meats, which he had providently brought out with him; and he now thinks it a good occasion to produce them. He accordingly puts the largest, labelled "mock-turtle, very rich," on the fire to cook; and seating himself upon an inverted water-bottle, proceeds to give me an animated account of his day's adventures. Rising suddenly, he is about to illustrate the exact position of a Kaffir he rather thinks he shot, when a loud explosion takes place, and some foreign body, which proves to be a lump of mock-turtle, hits him violently in the eye, and a shower of white soup, scalding hot, drenches his unhappy friend. The murder is out; and so is the mock-turtle. In his hurry he has not sufficiently regarded the written instructions, and has put the tin of soup on without first opening it. The fixed air beginning to expand under the genial influence of the fire, and finding no means of egress, in a rage reports the circumstance to my friend, who-rubbing his eye ruefully, expresses his disgust at tin meats in general; and our old friend Simpson thinks, as he chuckles to himself in his dry way, that "the mock-turtle warn't labelled *rich* for nothing." This was not so unfortunate, however, as his first essay in coffee-making in the field, on which occasion, having provided himself with the roasted beans, he put them into a kettle of boiling water, under the idea that he was making coffee. It turned out, I believe, excellent bean soup, but considered as coffee, was certainly a failure.

As it often happens, when there is nothing else to be had on patrol, the cow, from whose wretched carcass I get my rations, is very old and tough, and the meat, as it is brought hot and quivering from the newly-slaughtered beast, looks anything but tempting. Simpson, however, being an old hand, makes a very decent *carbonatgie* out of it, notwithstanding. This mode of dressing meat is very simple: first beating it well to make it tender, it is seasoned with pepper, and salt, then cut into long strips, it is twined round a stick and fixed into the ground at a proper angle over the fire. When eaten hot, it is excellent. Meat just killed may be dressed in this way and becomes eatable, however tough.

Night is now drawing on, and huge fires are blazing in every direction.

A camp at night is a most picturesque object. The various groups partially lit up by the blaze of the bivouac fire, the lively effect of the scarlet coat, contrasted with the pitchy darkness around; the incessant hum and buzz of a thousand voices, the shrieking laughter of the light-hearted Hottentot, joined to the shrill neighing of horses, and a multitude of other indescribable noises, with the flitting about of phantom-looking figures shrouded in mist, give one more the idea of pandemonium than anything else. By-and-by the hum ceases, the tired soldiers drop off to slumber, the fires, no longer fed, flicker and languish, bodies, swathed from head to foot in blankets, lie about by the dull embers, as if craving burial. The pale moon slowly rises and the camp is hushed in sleep. Sentries shrouded in blankets stalk noiselessly about, and were it not for the horses, which are perpetually trampling and fighting, the silence would be perfect. But there is no rest for them, nor do they seem inclined to afford it to any one within their range. It is as much as the sentries can do, by perpetually shouting and thrashing, to prevent them from tearing each other to pieces.

Two-thirds of the horses in Kaffir-land are entire. They are the greatest plague possible, fight desperately, and are always getting into mischief. I have my tent pitched just in rear of the line, and having struggled out of my coat and boots (for no one can be said to take off anything in a patrol-tent) have rolled myself up in my blankets and am just dropping off into a sweet slumber, when I am suddenly aroused by a terrible shock, and find a pair of equine hind legs intruding themselves into my tent, and ascertain on examination that the sentry having fallen asleep, the whole line of troopers has backed bodily upon me, and in another moment will demolish me altogether. Thoroughly awakened to the peril of my position, I charge out of my tent with a shout, on all fours, like a young behemoth, and away goes the line of horses in full retreat, or rather advance, carrying away with it all my loose ropes and standing rigging. It takes Simpson a good half hour to put these things to-rights, and I stand in the meantime without my stockings, and shivering in the wet grass.

I am aroused at four o'clock the next morning in a drizzling rain, refresh my inner man with a cup of lukewarm water and coffee-grounds, make frantic efforts, with my body doubled up, to pull on my boots, which I find lying near the door of my tent saturated with dew, and the column again moves off in the dark. We fall in with a few head of cattle, which are secured by the mounted men after a good deal of hard riding, and turn out to be the refuse of a larger herd, the better part of which have been already driven away, in anticipation, in another direction, by the Kaffirs.

We toil on through rugged passes, only to be traversed by means of cattle paths of the roughest kind, are waylaid in some villainous place by hordes of crouching foes, who, creeping up stealthily, discharge their deadly shafts from behind some sheltering bush, and retire as quickly as possible to reload, and so keep up a perpetual guerrilla warfare, harassing and destructive to the troops, who, packed in dense columns, offer every advantage to the arms of the assailants, whilst the latter are unseen and scattered.

The loss of the troops in this kind of campaigning is very great, nor is there any substantial advantage to show for it. From the nature of the country and the uncertainty of their position, few bodies of slain Kaffirs are ever discovered; whilst our losses have on some occasions amounted to between seventy and eighty killed and wounded during the operations of a single patrol.

We bivouac again at nightfall, the men tired and worn out with fatigue, not the slightest being the carriage of their dead and wounded on stretchers along the rough roads; it being a point of honour in Kaffir warfare that the bodies of the dead should be carried off the field by their comrades, that they may not be subjected to the mutilation and barbarous treatment of the savages, who not unfrequently cut the heads off as an offering to their prophet Umlangeni, with which to perform his mystic incantations.

When we wish to take cattle, or *surprise* any particular line of country, the plan is to travel during the night, or very early in the morning, and with this object the troops often accomplish fifteen or twenty miles before daybreak. All their movements are conducted with the greatest silence and secrecy; not a whisper is heard. The difficulty is to restrain the coloured part of the expedition from spoiling everything by their chattering. A Hottentot cannot travel ten yards without doing something. He must be talking, or striking his flint to light his pipe, or getting off every now and then to pick up something he has dropped; nevertheless, on a night march he behaves himself pretty well. The column now moves on, like a spectral procession, at a slow walk, in the most dreadfully dreary manner possible.

There are many more pleasant wanderings than a night march. The cold, the slowness of the pace, the monotonous tread of the men, all incline one irresistibly to slumber. It is sometimes the most difficult thing in the world, under all these influences, to keep awake. Even the hardy parchment-stained Hottentot dons his woollen night-cap and, clapping his forage cap upon the top of it, resigns himself to slumber. It is painful to watch him, oscillating like a pendulum, as he rolls about in his saddle, always managing to wake up with a choke, just in time to discover his danger, as he all but overbalances himself, first on one side and then on the other. The unfortunate subaltern, wrapped up in his blanket-coat, or *poncho*, fares no better, and everybody is a-nodding in delightful concert. It need hardly be observed that the practice of going to sleep on horseback is not unattended with danger.

The dawn is just breaking, and the column, having marched some sixteen or seventeen miles, at last approaches the long-expected *kraals*. We advance noiselessly, and have already surprised one herd of twenty head, which are still penned up in their *kraal*, when the Kaffirs unfortunately escape from the huts and give the alarm. Whoop after whoop echoes from the hills, and herds of cattle are seen moving off in all directions in the distance.

Now is the exciting time! The fun commences—away scamper the mounted men in full cry. some in one direction and some in another, each party with a herd in view, rattling along at full gallop, leaving the infantry to follow as best they can. As they near the herds, the Kaffirs redouble their exertions, and try to stimulate the panting oxen by shouting and firing their guns behind them. But it is of no avail; the *green coats* are upon them, and away they go into the bushes, now only intent upon their own safety.

The day has hardly broken and the column has captured some four or five hundred head of cattle, and everybody is in high spirits as they drive our spoil back, and think about breakfast. The sun rises hot and glowing; we have hardly halted two hours, yet the hills all around us are covered with Kaffirs, visibly increasing in number, and only waiting until the column shall move on to flock down and oppose its progress through the pass with our captured treasures.

It is nearly midday, and the Kaffirs, with their dusky columns still crown the heights, still watching and increasing in numbers. At length the advance is sounded, and the column slowly wends its way back, driving the bellowing oxen in its train. They are entrusted to the Fingoes, who surround them on all sides, and urge them on by shouts, in the centre of the column, and now the Kaffirs, gradually leaving the hills, disappear in the bushes, and it is perfectly well understood are making their way towards the column.

The road winds up a steep hill, flanked on one side by a ravine, and on the other by a dense bush. Presently a black body is seen creeping up through the bushes in the rear, then another, and the scrimmage begins. The column is hotly pressed as it ascends the hill, and there is soon a cry for stretchers, as man after man comes wounded from the rear. So the column toils on, halting every now and then where it can, and rushing back driving the Kaffirs before it. Moving on again, as hotly pursued by the savages, until it crowns the height and begins to descend the steep on the other side, where a fierce fire is kept up from a deep ravine on the left flank, into which no skirmishers can penetrate; but in which the wary Kaffir has, nevertheless, by means of a circuitous route, taken up his position, and is sending his fire into the column, which moves on through the pass as quickly as possible, returning volley after volley at random into the bushes at an unseen foe, and carrying off triumphantly its horned treasure, every score purchased with a life.

In this manner does the patrol accomplish its seven or fourteen days' tour, with an officer or two, besides some twenty or thirty men, killed and wounded, and as an equivalent some 400 or 500 lean cattle, perhaps none! And thus does patrol after patrol set out, enduring all kinds of hardships, and suffering continual loss of life, apparently without bringing the war one tittle nearer to its conclusion.

CHAPTER 13

Kaffir Warfare—the Boema Pass

The episodes which will now be given will, I hope, present to the reader a tolerably accurate notion of the harassing nature of Kaffir warfare, and show how materially it differs from that of civilised nations. I may recall, for this purpose, our first patrol or armed reconnaissance, which, I must premise, was planned when rumours of war were spreading over the country, more for the purpose of impressing our astute enemies with its warlike display, and showing them that we were on the alert, than with any idea of the probability of an attack on their part. For, in spite of the repeated warnings of old colonists, who saw the signs of war impending, so confident were the authorities, and so possessed with the unlikelihood of such an occurrence, that the officers in command had received the most stringent orders to restrain the troops from firing under any pretence, unless compelled to do so for the purpose of self-defence.

The force, consisting of about 200 Cape Mounted Rifles and three companies of infantry, left Graham's Town on the eve of Christmas day, 1851, with the intention of making a wide detour through the disaffected districts (a sort of royal progress in fact), and advanced on its way without obstruction as far as the Boema Pass, which forms the entrance to our military position at Keiskamma Hoek, in the heart of the Amatola Mountains.

Here we halted for breakfast, some Kaffirs, who lived in a hut near our bivouac, having supplied us with milk, etc., in the most friendly manner. The pass is very romantic, winding through a delightful park-like country, crossed by rapid streams of clear ice-cold water, and as it narrows becomes quite precipitous, the road dwindling to a mere footpath, so narrow that the mounted men could not ride more than two abreast, and is flanked on the precipice side by loose masses of rock intermingled with trees and bush, tangled with monkey-ropes and creepers of all kinds. The lower side slopes suddenly with a fall of about sixty feet to the bottom of the valley, where ran a rapid mountain stream which, gurgling as it rushed over its rocky bed, fell soothingly on the ear with a most refreshing sound.

As we rode on laughing and chatting I was just remarking to Dr. Stewart of my regiment, who was riding by my side in the rear of the troops, "What a jolly place it would be for a picnic, with shade and good water at hand," when an excited Hottentot soldier drew my attention to a strange circumstance.

Here and there at intervals along the roadside large boulders of rock had been placed with mathematical precision, each supporting a smaller stone symmetrically balanced on its summit. This ominous arrangement was evidently regarded by the native soldiers as a species of enchantment, invented by the great Kaffir prophet, Umlangeni, for the purpose of working mischief to the expedition, and the appearance of a Kaffir scout standing on the top of a mass of rock in an elevated position on the other side of the pass, from which he withdrew hastily on being discovered, was considered by them as proof positive of their surmises.

I was beginning to feel anxious, when Dr. Stewart's soldier-servant, riding hurriedly up, told him that the pack had slipped off his packhorse, which was in the rear of the column, and he at once rode off to see to it. Poor Stewart! I never saw him alive again!

At this moment we were startled by the sound of a heavy dropping fire from the rear, followed after an interval, by what we could detect as a volley of musketry from the infantry. Alas! this interval, fatal to many valuable lives, was caused by the halt of the infantry, who were obliged to wait whilst they loaded their muskets (this precaution having been considered quite unnecessary). Taken at a disadvantage, and thrown into confusion by the unexpected attack, they were now retiring at the double in complete disorder as the field-adjutant of the day, Major Bissett (now General Sir Jno. Bissett, K.C.M.G.), came galloping by on his way to the rear to discover the causes of the alarm.

The Cape Mounted Rifles were at once ordered to dismount and scatter into the bush. Being excited and somewhat tired of inaction, a brother officer, young Kingsley, and myself started off down the pass to try and recover a horse laden with ammunition, which was galloping wildly about wounded, and had advanced some distance when we met one of our European sergeants who called out to us that poor Dr. Stewart had been shot, and that we must not attempt to go any further as the pass was full of Kaffirs. Just at this moment, spurring on his horse, came Major Bissett, sitting upright by an effort on saddle, but from the traces of blood which marked his track and his ashen face, evidently badly wounded. He entreated us to follow and support him, so we had no alternative but to return. Major Bisset managed to get as far as the top of the pass, when he fell from his horse exhausted, and would have soon bled to death, a ball having pierced the femoral artery on one side, passing out through the other thigh in its course, had not Captain Carey fortunately happened, by a strange chance, to have brought a couple of handy little web tourniquets with him in his pouch-belt, which were immediately applied and the bleeding stopped.

In this attack three officers were wounded, and some twenty or thirty men left dead in the pass, whose bodies it was not considered possible, from the smallness of our force, to recover. From behind us came the triumphant yells of the Kaffirs, who in a moment seemed to fill the whole bush as we marched off discomfited to our camping ground some miles further on the plains. Will it be believed that when on the morrow we continued our route to Fort Cox, which was the nearest haven of shelter, the same orders to forbear from hostilities were repeated, on the supposition that the disaffection was limited to the particular tribe that had attacked us!

The column moved on as sorrowfully as might be. No Kaffirs made their appearance until we halted for breakfast on the top of a high hill, lined on either side with impenetrable bush, when we observed them in great numbers creeping along the jungle on our flank, with the evident intention of lining the road by which we were to pass. How we came to halt in such an exposed spot I cannot understand, especially as it gave the enemy plenty of time to make their arrangements to circumvent us. No sooner, however, did the column fall in and commence the descent on the other side, than we were once more trapped, and shot after shot came pouring in. Unable to see our enemy, and finding it impossible to make our way through the dense thorns, we were literally obliged to run the gauntlet and get out of it as best we could.

This second ambuscade, following as it did so quickly upon the heels of the first, caused quite a panic for the time, and a portion of the infantry did not in fact recover their morale for some time afterwards.

It may appear, perhaps, hardly credible to those who are unacquainted with the peculiarities of bush-fighting, that British troops should give way to panics of this description; but we must take into account that it is totally unlike civilised warfare.

In the first place the soldiers are accustomed to hear frightful accounts of the tortures to which prisoners who fall into the hands of the Kaffirs are subjected. Then again they are not practised sufficiently to act independently, but are so accustomed to closing up in rank that they get bewildered when they are scattered singly in the bush, and lose sight, if only for a time, of their companions, and cannot be made to understand that the only way to fight a native is to beat him with his own weapons and go into the bush, instead of remaining exposed in the open, where they are under every disadvantage. That once in the bush they are as good and better than the enemy, who is still more uneasy when he does not know where to expect his foe; it being a well-known axiom in Kaffir warfare, that so surely as our troops enter the bush, so surely do the Kaffirs make their exit on the other side. It is for these reasons that bush fighting is so distasteful to the regular soldier; and it is on the principle, perhaps, of set a thief to catch a thief, that the Hottentot is better fitted for the work.

The column having now rallied proceeded on its way, and the mounted men, opening out in the rear in skirmishing order, had as much as they could do to keep at bay the hosts of Kaffirs who now swarmed like bees, and were constantly trying to creep round our flanks. It was wonderful to see them skirmishing; taking advantage of every trifling inequality in the ground and bush, however small, which afforded the least cover. I have seen them drop down at full length behind an ant-heap, a puff of smoke as they fired being the only indication of their whereabouts. We had to make repeated charges to prevent their closing in on the column.

It was Christmas Day, but the weather was so intensely hot that the varnished peak of my forage cap actually melted, and ran dripping down on my nose, and I well remember halting for a moment beside a small *vley*, or pool, which had dried into liquid mud of a pea-soup colour and consistence, and thinking, as I drained the delicious compound out of a tin cup, that I had never enjoyed anything so much.

As we passed through a mimosa covered flat, which traversed the main road, I was riding in front with the advanced guard, when I encountered a horrible sight. Stretched out in fantastic positions across the path, lay the bodies of thirteen infantry soldiers in hideous array, horribly mutilated, the agony expressed in their glassy, upturned eyes showing that they had met with a lingering death by the sharp *assegais* of the Kaffirs. Painful experience has since taught me that this peculiar horror of expression always attends death when produced by sharp weapons in contradistinction to bullet wounds; a man shot through the head, for instance, presenting a perfectly peaceful appearance, as if overtaken by sleep. These unfortunate soldiers, as we afterwards learned, were sent to guard some wagons laden with stores on their way to Fort Cox. The careless escort thinking there was no danger, instead of being on the alert, were mostly riding in the wagons, the rest lagging behind, when they were surprised. The bodies had been evidently placed as we saw them by the Kaffirs for display, as an earnest that theirs was at least no temporising policy. The thought must have struck many of us as we picked up the poor fellows and made preparations for carrying them off, with a view to pay them the last sad honours on arrival, that our Christmas Day had been anything but a merry one!

On reaching Fort Cox we learnt the unwelcome news that war had broken out all over Kaffir-land, and that intelligence had just been received of the destruction of Auckland, one of our military villages, which had been surprised whilst the invalided soldiers, of whom it was composed, were off their guard and engaged in celebrating their Christmas festivities. It seems they had been overpowered and driven into their huts, which were then set on fire by their relentless enemies and the occupants burnt alive, Captain Armitage, who was in charge, fortunately escaping to the nearest settlement.

CHAPTER 14

Kaffir Warfare—a Hand to Hand Encounter

On another occasion a column of my regiment, with a detachment of infantry, was patrolling across country to carry out some intended movement. All at once we perceived a little knot of horsemen advancing towards us at full speed enveloped in a cloud of dust. They turned out to be a party of our native levies, who, as soon as they could get breath, informed us that they had just left a detachment of Cape Mounted Rifles commanded by Lieutenant Robertson, in a *kloof* some miles distant, where they had been surprised by Kaffirs, and as they grotesquely phrased it "cut up into little pieces by their *assegais*."

The order was given by Colonel G. Napier to ride off at once in pursuit, the levies undertaking to guide us, and the excitement was very great. Leaving the infantry to follow, a sharp gallop of some twenty minutes brought us to the brink of a steep *kloof*, where the encounter was said to have taken place, and we were no sooner dismounted and peering into the valley which was densely covered with mimosa bush, than we were aware of a cloud of Kaffirs who were hastily retreating, keeping up a scattered fire as they went.

Pat Robertson, a jovial reckless sub., was a universal favourite in the regiment, and we were all in great anxiety as to his fate. Looking over to the ascent on the opposite side of the ravine which was very steep, I perceived what I took to be Robertson, (he had a habit of wearing his trousers tucked into his long boots, which peculiarity was shared in by the figure before me) who appeared to be raising himself upon his elbow, as if beseeching assistance. Under this impression, I ran quickly down the sides of the ravine, and outstripping my companions, jumped over the ditch at the bottom, when my attention was arrested by the sight of the body of poor Fletcher, the adjutant of the 73rd foot, who was lying on his back with the shaft of an *assegai* protruding from his skull, where it had been left by his savage foes, and completely covered with spear wounds. So mutilated was he, that I only discovered his identity by picking up a notebook which he had dropped on the grass containing his name.

Leaving him where he lay, I hastened on. The figure I had seen proved to be the body of a Cape Rifleman, who, lying dead on the steep incline, had by a ghastly sort of optical illusion, the appearance of being alive, and in the act of rising. Hard by lay the bodies of several Kaffirs; one huge fellow had taken refuge in a mimosa bush, over one of the boughs of which he had fallen in the most grim fashion, his head and heels touching. He had an enormous bullet wound in his forehead, large enough to put one's fist into, showing what a close affair it must have been.

We learned afterwards from Pat Robertson, that he had set out from the adjoining camp accompanied by seven or eight Cape Mounted Rifles and levies to capture some Kaffir horses which they had perceived tied up to a bush at some distance. This was a snare, and by the time he had taken possession of them, the whole country was alive with Kaffirs. Overwhelmed by numbers they had retreated, and being compelled to cross the ravine, were obliged to dismount fighting literally hand to hand, leading their horses down the steep incline. Poor Fletcher who had joined the expedition, received a shot in the knee which brought him to the ground. A Cape Mounted Rifleman was killed, and a young officer of levies, a mere lad, was badly wounded in the side by an *assegai*. Robertson's horse was shot, and the trooper, led by the young levy officer, being frightened, made his escape and he was on the point of being captured, when Robertson had the good fortune to catch the dead rifleman's horse, jumped on his back, and placing the young fellow across his saddle, made his escape back to the camp. The remainder made their way up the other side of the ravine, and were in full flight, when they fortunately encountered our column.

The bodies having been removed from the *kloof*, which was quite impracticable to cavalry, the order was given to move on. Quite unaware of the fact, I was slowly retiring up the steep side on my way to the top, with a staunch old Cape Mounted Rifle sergeant, when sundry dropping shots which fell around us, made us turn our heads; and we saw that the Kaffirs, aware of the retreat of the column, were returning in force through the scrub. At this moment Sergeant Exteen and myself sighted two fellows who had continued to keep up until a few yards below us, and were in the act of firing. However we anticipated this little manoeuvre, and filing rapidly had the satisfaction to see them fall; one of them was evidently a head man or chief of some kind, and wore a solid ivory armlet which I was desirous of possessing; but the huge brute made such awful faces, snapping his white teeth together in his dying agonies (my bullet having entered his chest) that I delegated the unpleasant task to the sergeant. He had just succeeded in drawing the armlet off, when we discovered that we were quite alone, and scrambling to the summit, perceived the column which had never missed us in full retreat. Happily, one of the mounted men had found our horses, and now led them up from an adjoining bush; we lost no time in mounting, and rode off at score amidst a perfect shower of missiles.

CHAPTER 15

Kaffir Warfare—a Ride for Life

Narrow escapes of the kind related in the preceding chapter were everyday occurrences. I remember that at another time, we were patrolling over a wide plateau dominating the Keiskamma river which wound at its base, and looking down its precipitous sides, we could perceive a small herd of cattle penned up in a *kraal* in the centre of a little bush-covered flat bordering the stream. Tired of the slow pace of the column, and longing for a gallop, Lieut. Whitmore and myself asked permission to go in pursuit. As cattle hunting is one of the great ends of Kaffir warfare, this was accorded; and three or four mounted men having volunteered to accompany us, we started, and at once set about looking for something in the shape of a path by which to descend the cliff, which formed at this part almost a sheer precipice of some three hundred feet. We made the descent by a rough cattle path, sending down showers of loose stones and debris before us, as the horses half-slid, half-scrambled to the base. I remember looking back to the scarcely perceptible track by which we had descended, and wondering how we had achieved it.

Winding through the dense thorns we soon found the *kraal*, and the men having collected together the cattle, we were puzzling our brains how to return. This was a poser. To ascend the cliff by the way we came was impossible; whilst on the other side ran the Keiskamma river, wide and deep. Clearly, the only way out of the difficulty, was to find a ford. We were diligently occupied in searching for one, when we perceived a mounted rifleman on the other side, who was gesticulating very excitedly, and evidently trying to warn us of some danger. As he was inaudible, one of the mounted men rode down to the bank, and reported that he was urging us to make our escape, as the bush behind us was full of Kaffirs.

The warning came not a whit too soon; within twenty yards of us, creeping through the bush in all directions, came a whole horde of naked savages, yelling and flourishing their guns and *assegais* in evident triumph at the success of their stratagem. Loudly shouting to the men who had lagged behind us, to warn them of their peril, we put our horses at full gallop along the borders of the river, anxiously looking out for any sign of a ford by which we might cross. It was a ride for life!

Fortunately, to our great joy, we hit upon a ford at last; but it was so close a shave, that by the time we reached the other side of the river by the ford—which was up to our horses' girths, and which we splashed through at a gallop, the Kaffirs had actually reached the bank we had left, and were only prevented from capturing the two men who had lagged behind by a well-sustained fire from our double-barrelled carbines. A baffled yell from the disappointed Kaffirs was answered by a cheer of triumph from our little party as we rode off. The soldier who had so providentially warned us, belonged to another division, which was carrying out a combined movement at a short distance, and had happily strayed by chance from his companions.

I could multiply instances without end of this kind of adventure, of which in truth a Kaffir campaign may be said to consist, rather than of any regular series of operations or combined movements on the part of the troops employed. These, together with long night marches, keeping us sometimes twelve or thirteen hours in the saddle, undertaken for the purpose of surprising the Kaffirs, and inflicting generally more loss of cattle than of human life upon the foe (who could always, if he wished, avoid coming to close quarters, and could watch his opportunity to get us entangled in some ambush or difficult position where the advantage was altogether on his own side), tended to prolong almost indefinitely the campaign, which dragged on its protracted existence for the space of three years, and was not terminated until 1853. The Kaffirs were then driven out of Kaffir-land, across the river Kei, which was their proper boundary.

Though the war brought no glory to our armies, nor any substantial benefit, it exposed our troops to continual fatigue and great privations. So exhausting was it, from the effects of protracted marches and constant exposure, that when it was concluded, the hospitals were full of strong, able-bodied men— prostrated by heart-disease and other complaints, which were aggravated by the unwholesome nature of the food—hard biscuit and meat, fresh-killed, with an almost entire absence of vegetables, being the only available diet in the field.

I can speak feelingly on the subject; the constant exposure to which we were subjected, having brought on a severe attack of rheumatism, which completely crippled me for some years, and was further aggravated by scurvy—the combined effect being to necessitate my going home to England to recruit, and eventually entailing my compulsory retirement from the service. I say this advisedly, as Adjutant-General Foster, on the plea that I had enjoyed too much sick-leave already, and that I must serve or sell, refused to confirm the recommendation of the medical board, under Dr. Logan, for another year's leave, which it had without hesitation accorded me. This decision, taking into consideration that I had acquired my disabilities in the field, and should have completed my fifteen years' service in four months' time, was exceedingly harsh treatment; more especially as it prevented my making up the fifteen years' service, which would have entitled me to half-pay; so that the best part of my life, and my fourteen years and eight months' service, were completely thrown away.

I protested, used all the means in my power, and memorialised over and over again, without effect; and although the late Lord Clyde applied on my behalf for an appointment as staff-officer of pensioners, it was refused to me on this very ground of not having completed the fifteen years' service, which was necessary to qualify me for that post. This is all I have gained from my military services, in despite of excellent testimonies from the different officers commanding my regiment.

I was sent down from King William's Town, just before the completion of the war, to Buffalo Mouth, to recruit my health and get the benefit of sea air. Here I had quarters allotted to me in the fort of that name, which was used as a station for the naval and marine officers belonging to the different vessels, which touched here for the purpose of transporting men and stores for the troops on the frontier. The station at this time included a deputy-commissary general and a staff-doctor, under whose auspices a most comfortable little mess was initiated. The friendly Kaffirs brought us in capital rock-oysters, packed up in wet moss, which we highly appreciated. These rock-oysters were well-flavoured and sweet, though not so symmetrical as our natives, being very irregular in shape and difficult to open. As my companions were, from constant practice, very adroit in this art, I was obliged to learn how to accomplish the feat in self-defence; and, finding my allowance falling short, soon became very expert.

The surf at Buffalo Mouth is most formidable—coming on shore in immense rollers, to cope with which it became necessary to employ massive boats measuring seventeen or eighteen tons, very solidly constructed; the warp or cable upon which they work being carried out to a considerable distance from the shore into smooth water, where it is securely attached to a heavy anchor. The warp itself passes over the boat fore and aft to the stern, being kept in its place by an iron pin. By hauling on this cable and warping up to the anchor, continual trips are made between the vessels and the shore, and stores and passengers landed. Notwithstanding all precautions, it is at best a service of danger, and before these large boats were constructed, accidents were of frequent occurrence; twenty-two seamen having been drowned within a comparatively short space of time— the undertow of the current inevitably drawing the poor fellows down, and leaving the best swimmers helpless. Before starting it is necessary to batten down the hatches, as the heavy sea continually washes over the decks. The passengers, who occupy the deck in preference to going down below, have to hold on when the boat encounters the surf; as the large volume of water, which attains a height of ten or twelve feet, comes on like an immense wall, and forces the boat straight up on end like a rearing horse, until it seems only prevented from falling completely over on the other side by the warp, so that one not on his guard is very likely to go overboard. The crew have to hold on like grim death, until the roller has passed underneath, and can only make play between the intervals.

Our principal amusements were quail-shooting and deep sea-fishing, which is very good; and off the rocks, as the tide came in, we caught fine rock-cod, and a very pretty species of sea-perch, of a silvery-white banded with black. The scenery at Buffalo Mouth is very picturesque, with considerable depth of stream, the banks being well-wooded down to the water's edge.

This place used some few years since to be a favourite haunt of the sea-cow or hippopotamus; Dr. Barclay, of the 91st regiment, shot a very fine specimen, the head of which he afterwards preserved in a very life-like manner. He had a very narrow escape of his life on the occasion. The sea-cow forces its way through the thick jungle in its passage from the river, foraging during the night upon the tender grass and succulent shrubs, and when startled always takes to the water for protection. Dr. Barclay was following the *spoor* of a sea-cow up one of these paths, when it became apparent that he had cut off the huge brute from its retreat. He had hardly time to throw himself down on his face (the bush being impenetrable on either side) before the monster came rushing along, actually passing over him as he lay in its course. Fortunately he was protected where he fell by an irregularity in the ground, which saved his life, and he afterwards followed up the animal, and by a lucky shot killed it. The body immediately sunk and drifted down the stream; but was eventually found by his Kaffir followers near the mouth of the river. The sea-cows have long since abandoned this part of the country and are now only to be found far up in the interior.

CHAPTER 16

The Sovereignty

Ox my return from a year's sick leave the English government had already determined to give up the Orange River Sovereignty to the Boers, finding it very unprofitable as a possession, from the constant embroilment of the settlers with the Basutos, and the expense of sending troops to protect a tract of country so distant. They appointed Sir Geo. Clerk, a well-known Indian officer, in conjunction with Commissioner Owen, who had some experience in the country, to proceed to Bloem Fontaine for the purpose of arranging the terms upon which the sovereignty was to be abandoned. Sir Geo. Clerk, who had a son in the Cape Rifle Regiment, kindly asking me if I would accompany him on the expedition, I gladly consented; and was accordingly detailed as officer commanding the mounted escort, which was to be furnished by my troop. As this trip would take me into some of the best parts of the game country I was proportionally delighted at the offer.

Behold us, then, setting out from the frontier capital (Graham's Town) with our cavalcade of ox wagons for the *impedimenta*, horse wagons for the staff (should they become tired of the saddle), the spare horses being led by our servants. Nothing can be more delightful in a beautiful climate than this independent mode of travelling. It is one continued picnic. Our day commences with a ride of seventeen or eighteen miles, terminating in breakfast already prepared under some friendly bush on our arrival by the Malay cook, who has been sent on in advance, and which consists, among other delicacies, of huge rashers of hippopotamus bacon (which, by-the-bye, I can recommend), supplemented with a species of mullet generally to be found in the rivers in this part.

Being fond of anything in the way of angling, I was, in contemplation of that sport, provident enough to carry with me a selection of medium-sized Limerick hooks, and a few gut traces, the line being improvised out of a ball of twine, and the sinkers supplied from our shot pouches, anything in the shape of a stick answering for a rod. Many a pleasant hour have I whiled away in this manner; the more interesting from the absolute uncertainty as to what manner of fish the bait would attract. There was no great variety; perhaps one's capture would be the mullet or a species of yellow carp, large scaled, and not very good eating, or a huge *barga* (evidently a *silurus*), with its monstrous head adorned with bristling feelers and scaleless eel-like body, rich flavoured and good for the table, running up to twelve or fourteen pounds in weight, and, I am told, even larger. At another time it might be an unfortunate terrapin (the fresh water tortoise) which had been lured from the muddy bottom by the fascinations of the red worm—the bait usually employed.

Our table was at times graced with a brace or two of the handsome wild ducks of which there are many varieties, though rarely met with on account of the scarcity of water in this arid country; or sometimes a succulent teal, with its delicate pink beak, or a gigantic moorhen, with its vivid white shirt-collar-like appendages, standing out in fine relief against its jetty plumage, would replace it. Sometimes we had the good luck to come upon a covey of red-legged partridges, which found excellent cover in the large tufts of wiry grass with which the streams are fringed. Here the difficulty would be to get them up, as they ran with such speed, that in the absence of dogs we could hardly keep pace with them. Fortunate indeed would we consider ourselves when we found the familiar gray partridge, or some of the many varieties of bustard; commencing with that magnificent bird the *paou*, or great bustard, with its beautiful cinnamon and gray speckled plumage, small game head and taper neck, weighing from sixteen to thirty pounds, but so wary that it is only to be got at in the *veldt*, by riding round it in circles, ever lessening until the happy moment when sufficiently near to get within shot. The huge bird, in the meanwhile, stupidly regards the horseman with turning neck, apparently fascinated by the manoeuvre; and then, what a delicious mixture of white and brown flesh when he came to table, the breast brown and gamey, and the wings and sides equal to the most delicious turkey.

Some of the smaller species fall at times an easy prey to the hunter, from the curious habit (common I believe to the bustard tribe) of poking their long necks into some little clump of grass or bush, and coolly awaiting his approach under the fallacious idea that they are invisible. The small black bustard or *koor haan*, when disturbed, mounts like the English pheasant to a great height, before he wheels off, uttering the most discordant cries, and so distinctly calls out *knock me down, knock me down*, that he goes by this title in the colony; the modest demand being cheerfully complied with by the two-legged enemy lying in wait for him. The large bustards may not unfrequently be easily approached in the breeding season, as they are in the habit of assembling together in considerable numbers, on the low rocky hills with which the vast plains are bounded. Even then a good lookout must be kept, as they rise on the wing so noiselessly that their flight is quite imperceptible to any sense but the sight. I have in this way shot right and left with No. 1 shot, a brace weighing twenty-five and twenty pounds.

On this occasion I was accompanied by my soldier servant, who was riding my spare horse, the saddle upon which was already laden with one of the large bustards, and a brace and a half of the smaller kind, black and gray, as large as good-sized ducks, which he had firmly tied to the saddle D's with strong strips of untanned leather, called *reimpys*. The animal was a stubborn tempered, strong, useful pony, but very wilful;

and when we added insult to injury by fastening on the two enormous birds I had just shot, he waited until the operation was completed, and then, rapidly going round in circles, twisted the reins out of my servant's hands to his dismay, and galloped off, having first viciously thrown himself down on the ground with the intention of rolling off the birds; but, thanks to the strong fastenings, we found them on our arrival safely landed, notwithstanding their twelve miles homeward journey. The pony's appearance caused some alarm to my military companions, who, seeing him riderless, naturally thought that some accident had befallen his master.

We had progressed on our journey some six or seven hundred miles before we entered the habitat of the larger game for which the Cape is so famous. We had indeed lately come across small isolated herds of that beautiful antelope the springbok, with its pretty cinnamon-coloured coat, streaked on the sides with bars of white and chocolate, and, when bounding away at full speed, expanding the lovely snow wreath of white fur on its hind quarters. But this was as nothing to our delight on reaching the zone frequented by the larger game, where were vast herds of antelopes in beautiful variety, intermingled with zebras and ostriches, covering the plain and indiscriminately feeding in company. This is indeed a sight to delight the sportsman, and supplies the naturalist with endless amusement and instruction, as he examines unrestrainedly the different beauties and characteristics of each species.

Among the most singular is the gnu or wildebeest as the Boers term it. Of these strange antelopes I have counted as many as a thousand in a herd. It is a most grotesque anomalous creature, with its pony-like body, antelope legs, and buffalo-looking head, furnished with retreating curved horns and sinister deep sunken eyes and adding to the savage bristling bottle brush of hair standing erect upon its ox-like nose, a hogged mane striped with alternate bars of black and white—the *tout ensemble* finished off with a flourishing white tail, the erect hair upon which grows only on the upper side.

In addition to these peculiarities its habits are equally eccentric. When feeding on the plains, scouts are sent out from the herd to give timely notice in case of alarm. These sentinels (for they are nothing else) are generally the old bulls who stand about singly, facing outwards, and on the approach of any danger, stamp with their forefeet in the most petulant manner, whisk their sides with their tails, and give vent to a singular grunting bellow ending in a succession of squeaks of the most laughable kind; then execute a *gambado* in the air and canter off to warn their companions. Now ensue the most strange manoeuvres on the part of the main body. They start off at full speed, following each. other in exact Indian file, the head of the hindmost almost touching the tail of the foremost, until the whole herd forms a continuous line. This manoeuvre is continued till they are safe from pursuit, when the line breaks up suddenly and they begin cantering round each other, still in single file, circle within circle, in the most intricate patterns, flourishing their white tails in the air. So intensely ludicrous is their appearance, that I have seen one of my companions, unused to the sight, drop his rifle and roll on the ground in contortions of laughter, content to regard the singular spectacle to the utter oblivion of his original murderous intentions.

We have heard the old idea of eccentric people having "maggots in the brain," for which saying I believe the immortal Shakespeare is responsible. Strange to say, that eccentric animal the wildebeest may be put forward as an undoubted proof of the soundness of this theory. I have seen as many as seven large fat white maggots taken from a little membranous sack in the *periosteum*, lying close upon the brain of the beast, wriggling about in the most lively manner when extracted; and this too from a healthy specimen.

The wildebeest, however, is not the only animal afflicted in this manner. On passing the hand over the coat of the Vaal Raybok (a fine antelope found on the plains in the colony), it comes in contact with sundry movable lumps, plainly perceptible under the skin. These are caused by the presence of large maggots, which can be easily extracted alive from their hiding-places; and on this account the Boers refuse to eat the flesh of this handsome animal. I have seen many specimens of the Vaal Raybok, and they were always accompanied by this strange parasite.

The springbok herds, when disturbed, go off also in their own peculiar fashion. An *avant-garde* formed of two or three single bucks, precedes the rest at full speed, taking the most surprising leaps into the air in succession, and are followed by their companions *en masse*. Then come racing on the blessboks and hartebeests, with their long swinging stride. The zebras collect together in small herds of from ten to twenty, and with their striped bodies when in motion, present a most peculiar indistinct blurred appearance, as if seen through the influence of a mirage.

The ostriches go off singly at incredible speed; their flight in some measure assisted by their rudimentary wings, which they carry outstretched, taking them along at a hopeless rate, as far as horse speed is concerned; their stride from footprint to footprint often giving a good measured thirty feet. Many a time I have tried, unsuccessfully, even with a horse going at racing speed, to cut them off by riding to a point. It is hopeless. The Boers have a way of tiring them out, by following them up all day, at just sufficient speed to enable them to keep within sight; but this would be too tedious for the ordinary sportsman.

CHAPTER 17

The Ostrich

The ostrich has now become a considerable object of enterprise at the Cape; ostrich-farming having been introduced, and being sometimes profitable. The white feathers are only found in the male bird; the female being more humbly clad in sombre brown plumes, which are of so little value that they are hardly worth plucking, as far as commerce is concerned.

The ostrich farms are simply large tracts of *veldt* enclosed within wire or other fencing, a very slight obstruction being sufficient to keep the birds from straying. The eggs are hatched either in incubators or by the parent birds; the artificially developed chickens being quite as healthy as those hatched in the natural way. Eggs taken in the desert are thus utilized. At five years' old the birds are paired, the young ones being kept in flocks.

The ostriches peck up a quantity of sand and pebbles in the *veldt*, which helps them to digest their food. The young birds are very tame, but the more matured often very fierce. The feathers produced by the tame bird are quite equal in quality to those taken from the wild birds. As the demand for ostrich feathers is always in excess of the supply, the profits from a properly-conducted farm are very great; an ostrich a few months old being worth from £60 to £100, as it yields about seven pounds' worth of feathers when a year old; and an increasingly valuable supply every nine months.

I once had a curious adventure with an ostrich. I was riding across the flats unarmed, when I perceived a Boer jump out of his ox wagon at some distance, and kneeling down, take a pot-shot at something. Looking in the direction of the line of fire, I observed a fine male ostrich, accompanied by a female, which were just going over a low hill on the right, and were almost in line. The Boer fired at the male, which was a little in advance, and missed it, hitting the female; and they both disappeared over the ridge. Anxious to see the effect of the shot, I rode up. The Boer, finding that he had missed the cock bird, jumped into his wagon again, sending his bush-boy after the wounded female to pick out some of her less valuable feathers. Riding over the hill, I perceived the female (evidently badly hit), at a little distance, on a rocky bit of ground near a small clump of bush, where it had taken refuge. The bush-boy was standing a little way off, afraid to approach nearer, as the gigantic bird, though brought to the ground with a broken leg, looked very formidable. Giving him my horse to hold, I dismounted, and walking up to the bird, gave it a smart rap on the head with a *sjambok* (a heavy whip of rhinoceros hide) that I carried, and to my astonishment, killed it instantaneously. The skull must have been very thin for such a blow to have been fatal. I was struck by the enormous size and power of the thigh and legs of the ostrich, and can well believe that a blow from this formidable limb might break a man's leg or arm, as is said to be the case. The boy contented himself with plucking a few of the brown feathers, and had already abandoned the fallen foe as I rode off.

The natives sometimes brought us in ostrich eggs, which they had found on the flats; and these we found excellent when made into omelettes, the yolk being rich and well-flavoured, and one egg supplying an abundant meal for five or six persons. The Hottentots have an ingenious method of carrying the ostrich eggs away from the nest in the *veldt*. Taking off their trousers, they stuff the eggs into the legs of that garment, tying the spaces between them with a flexible grass, and throwing the sacks thus made over their shoulders. In this fashion they manage to carry them safely; an undertaking which their slippery surfaces and unaccommodating form, would otherwise render very difficult.

The nest is nothing more than a shallow depression scraped in the sandy soil with their powerful feet; the cock and hen birds sitting on the eggs alternately until matured. If once disturbed, the birds destroy the eggs and abandon the nest. The flesh is not considered eatable, and the ostrich has therefore no value apart from its feathers.

The flats frequented by these vast herds of game are of enormous extent, and are covered with a wiry kind of grass, called *suur veldt* (sour grass), with occasional patches of *karoo* bush, quite destitute of anything in the shape of a tree, and, with the exception of a few scattered farms, void of population. Nothing can be more dreary than a night passed in the *veldt*, where the only sounds are the distant roar of the lion, the piercing screams of the jackal, or the demoniacal laugh of the spotted hyena, as it prowls stealthily round the encampment; but daylight dispels all illusions; and as you watch the vast horizon, and regard the varied troops of antelopes careering over the plains in their freedom and beauty, you bless the chance which has brought you into this paradise of sportsmen.

The officers belonging to the 45th Regiment, who had been stationed here for many years, were great nimrods. Colonel Kyle, the Lieutenant-Colonel commanding, was a most successful lion-hunter, a first-rate rifle shot, and could pick off the single wildebeest bulls at three hundred yards with beautiful precision. He had killed no less than thirteen lions at different times on his sporting trips up the country, trekking with his wagon long distances into the interior for the purpose. My companions being therefore quite accustomed to the large game-shooting, kindly put me up to many a wrinkle, and thus I fortunately had every chance to commence my operations in the field with success. They had a comfortable little mess, and it was very pleasant to meet after the day's sport, and talk over our adventures.

This mess-house had a little stone *stoep*, or veranda, to the beams of which might be seen suspended a long row of water-bottles, enveloped in wet cloths and exposed to the draught, which was a simple method of turning them into refrigerators; and from this *coign of 'vantage*, which looked over the wide Bloem Fontaine flats, the town being built upon a gentle eminence, we could always see one or more distant herds of antelopes, showing as dark specks in the prairie, the presence of which in any particular spot often determined the direction of our day's hunting.

In the sultry weather, the plains were often covered with mirage, and positively glowed with heat, which radiated off the warm earth in flickering vapour, just as one sees it over a lime-kiln. The mirage itself was a beautiful object, enveloping the desert in long sheets of white mist, which not only took the forms here and there of distant lakes and streams, but often had the effect of inverting the far hills and living objects in a most extraordinary manner, reflecting them above the horizon, so that it was difficult to say where the earth ended and the sky began.

CHAPTER 18

Bloem Fontaine

Bloem Fontaine is as desolate a looking place as it is possible to imagine, being situated on a plain almost destitute of vegetation, surrounded by low chains of stony *kopjies* (small hills), and consisting principally of a long rambling main street, where stands conspicuous the bam-like Dutch reformed church, with the wooden stores, or *winkels*, belonging to the general merchants, mostly German Jews, who supply the country round with all kinds of miscellaneous articles, nothing coming amiss to them, from a Jew's harp to a grand piano.

These men, by their thrifty habits and business aptitude, are among the most prosperous and respectable of the Cape colonists in the interior. They are very clannish, and seldom make their way in the world, and form comfortable homes without sending for their poorer kindred from the fatherland and bestowing upon them a share of their prosperity; and I must say, from my own personal experience, that I have always met with the greatest hospitality from them. They are well educated, as a rule, and very intelligent; the ladies especially are generally charming in person and unassuming in manner, very superior indeed to the men in refinement and personal appearance. The German Jews, probably from their wandering proclivities and Eastern origin, seem to take kindly to the colonies, where they settle down quite easily and naturally, seldom moving when they are once fixed, and adding much, by their solid qualities and energy, to the prosperity of the settlements in which they reside.

The English Church, placed as it is on an eminence overlooking the town, forms a prominent object at Bloem Fontaine. Scattered here and there about the plain are the pretty little cottages of the settlers, each surrounded by its fringe of green foliage, the gardens filled with flowers and fruit trees, amongst which the peach orchards are conspicuous.

The peach trees are never trained against the walls as with us, but are planted in rows like standard apple trees, and are generally loaded with a profusion of fruit, beautifully coloured and exceedingly fine, but far inferior in flavour to our wall-fruit. The fruit is so plentiful as to be scarcely of any value, but is very refreshing in the sultry climate. Oranges grow also to great perfection, and a variety of grapes are cultivated. I tasted in the residents' garden most delicious muscatels and sweet-water grapes, with crystal honey-pot and other kinds, which grow most luxuriantly.

Here and there amongst the settlers' houses are scattered little colonies of Kaffir huts, which give shelter to sundry families of wandering Basutos; the approach to which may always be discovered by the numerous heads and debris of wildebeest and other antelopes, which lie kicking about half buried in the sand.

I was strolling about on the flat and had reached the low hills on the outskirts of the settlement, when I became aware of a collection of reed huts, more squalid than usual. They were composed of a slight framework of sticks, planted in the ground and curved over so as to meet on the top, and were only partially covered with scanty patches of reeds soddened and rotting in places and full of holes, the interstices being patched up with sundry disreputable looking skins of oxen and antelopes—the blue smoke escaping not only from the low doors but from innumerable crevices in the dilapidated thatch. Crawling nervelessly about in the neighbourhood of the huts, were sundry decrepit Kaffirs, who mumbled out some undistinguishable words in a peculiar hoarse, whistling voice. On regarding them more minutely, I was much struck with their appearance. None of them possessed their proper complement of limbs. One had a foot missing, another a hand wanting as far as the wrist, and another again a portion of his face imperfect. These disfigurements had something unaccountable in their character which quite took them out of the category of ordinary accidents or mutilation; the stumps where the limbs were wanting, for instance, had the appearance of rotting away by a species of dry decay, as there had been apparently no effusion of blood. The *cicatrices* presented invariably a bluish powdery surface, and the thought suddenly flashed across me, "they are lepers;" and here, no doubt, being obliged to come out from amongst their brethren, they were allowed to retreat, eking out their miserable existence as human outcasts and pariahs.

This, I was informed, was the case. They were fed by compassionate friends, who paid them occasional visits for the purpose, but were otherwise quite isolated and alone. They crawled up to my feet, begging in the most abject manner for tobacco. *"Bazaala tobaka,"* they cried. I gave them what I could spare out of my pouch, and was only too glad to make my escape, shuddering, from the unhallowed spot. I had heard of the existence of a leper hospital in one of the villages in the neighbourhood of Cape Town, but had never visited it. I understand that there is no cure for this hideous malady, nor do their sufferings admit of much alleviation. It is probably more vegetation than life, and there is every reason to hope that nature, which fits the back to the burden, so blunts their faculties, mental and bodily, as to make their wretched condition more tolerable than might be supposed.

The block composing the infantry and cavalry barracks at Bloem Fontaine, was the merest collection of mud huts; the officers living in little detached cottages near. But these and other discomforts were cheerfully put up with, the magnificent sport in this splendid game country making amends for all drawbacks.

My first essay after large game was made upon a small herd of zebras, which we had surprised upon a flat some miles from the settlement. A young commissariat officer, who was an ardent sportsman, having undertaken to initiate Sir George Clerk's son and myself in the mysteries of large-game shooting, we set out on the first opportunity for that purpose. When some miles had been accomplished, on emerging from a narrow pass formed by the approach of the low hills, we perceived the indistinct outlines of a small herd of zebra.

"Now," said our commissariat friend, "we must' try to cut them off by riding at full speed, as our only chance of getting near is to breathe them; if allowed to go their own pace we shall never get within shot."

Following our instructions off we went, *at score*, and soon found ourselves nearing the herd. When about two hundred yards off, my companions, unable to restrain their ardour, jumped off their horses and took pot-shots, missing them *handsomely*. Seeing, however, that I was rapidly shortening the distance, I kept going, and soon had the satisfaction of coming up so completely alongside the hindermost, that, pointing my smooth-bore loaded with ball, almost touching his body behind the shoulders, I dropped him instantaneously. This plan I afterwards successfully adopted when zebra shooting. On one occasion, indeed, so close was I to my zebra, that my pony had to jump over his prostrate body in his stride, which he did most cleverly, the zebra having fallen immediately under his nose. The bullet entered just under the root of the tail, the gun being held pointing between the pony's ears.

I remember, on this occasion, trying to skin the zebra, having dismounted for this purpose, and, in the absence of assistance, tying the wilful pony by his leather *reim* to the zebra's head. Having succeeded with much labour in skinning one side, I found that the beast was too heavy for me to turn over, and at the same time the pony was beginning to tug at the *reim*. I was obliged to abandon all thoughts of getting the skin, and content myself with cutting off the tail and a part of the mane as trophies, which I had the greatest difficulty in carrying away, the pony strongly objecting to my mounting encumbered with these *impedimenta*.

The Boers sometimes shoot the female zebra when with

young, and perform the Caesarean operation, cutting out the embryo, which, with its handsomely marked satin skin, is soon converted into a gorgeous waistcoat. I once, by chance, shot a female under these circumstances, and, being anxious to see the embryo, took it from the dead mother. It was a beautiful object, perfectly formed even down to its delicate little blue hoofs, and the texture of the striped skin was quite silky. I was sorry that I had no means of preserving it.

The zebra of the plains is the variety known as Burchell's zebra. The ground colour of the hide is a rich orange yellow, and it differs also from the mountain or true zebra, in the marking of the stripes, which is not continued down the legs as in the zebra proper. The Boers try to utilize it by training it to harness, which, from its strong, compact make, it would seem to be well fitted for; but it is irreclaimably wild, and kicks and bites so determinedly, that it is impossible to civilize it.

Two companies of infantry and a troop of Cape Mounted Rifles were at this time stationed at Bloem Fontaine, and the great ambition of those officers at headquarters, who were fond of shooting, was to be sent here on duty, the parades being almost nominal, and the allowance of forage so ample, especially in the case of the Cape Mounted Rifle officers, that it was quite sufficient to keep as many horses as were required on these enormous plains. A good stud is a necessity; for frequently the *veldt* stretches seventy miles without anything larger than a bush, and the pursuit of such shy game on foot is, from the nature of the ground, a matter of impossibility.

Apropos to this subject I remember an unfortunate staff doctor (an Irishman) coming up from headquarters full of ardour, having succeeded in negotiating an exchange with a brother medico of non-sporting tendencies, and I fancy I even now see his face beaming with delight when, on nearing his destination at Bloem Fontaine, he first caught sight of the vast herds of antelopes sporting over the plains. As soon as he could unpack his gun and ammunition, and without waiting for the escort of his more experienced brethren, he set off, accompanied only by his bushman servant, riding a spare horse, eager for the chase. He had not ridden far before he discovered to his delight a fine herd of blessbok careering in front of him. Off he went at full gallop, followed by his after-rider; but, alas! *there is many a slip between the cup and the lip,* for his horse, which was untrained, suddenly encountered in his course a nest of meerkat holes—a nimble little animal of the *ichneumon* tribe which lives gregariously like the prairie dog in burrows made in the sandy ground so close together that it is completely honeycombed with them, and so rotten that it crumbles away upon the slightest pressure. The horse, seeing its danger, suddenly swerved off at an acute angle, and its unfortunate rider swerving off at another acute angle, fell heavily to the ground, breaking his forearm just below the elbow. The bush boy picked him up in a very bad state, and got him home as quickly as he could by leading his horse, *miscrabile dictum.* This was his first essay and his last at the big game; for by the time the bones of his arm were sufficiently set to make the limb once more serviceable, his term of leave had expired, and he was once more, to his infinite disgust, compelled to pack up his traps and set off on his return to headquarters.

When Sir George Clerk first arrived at Bloem Fontaine, the whole district was suffering from one of those fearful droughts which form the great drawback to this otherwise fine country. Scarcely any rain had fallen for nearly nine months, and the English colonists were much annoyed that the high commissioner should have the misfortune to see their settlement under such unfavourable circumstances. It had in fact, as they grandiloquently termed it in their *Bloem Fontaine Gazette,* arrived at its "culminating point of sterility." So parched was it becoming day by day, that the *karoo* bush and wiry grass which formed the chief subsistence of the vast herds of game, had perished down to the very roots, and the antelopes were retreating in great numbers further into the interior, where water was more abundant.

To add to their miseries, a most unprecedented shower of sleety snow fell continuously, for the space of three days. So fatal did this prove to the animals inhabiting the plains, that I actually saw wildebeests and other antelopes make their way blindly into the middle of the town in search of shelter, where they were easily captured. After the storm ceased, they were found dying in all directions, and the plains were covered with their carcasses. In the course of an afternoon's ride, I counted as many as seventy dead antelopes of all species. I was told that ostriches even were found amongst the slain. The hideous asvogels or common vultures were so gorged that they cared only to tear out the eyes here and there, as a kind of *bonne bouche*, leaving the bodies otherwise unmolested. The bodies presented a curious sight; decomposition had so far set in that they were enormously swollen and inflated.

The herds which had managed to escape the scourge were so weak and ran so feebly, that it would have been rank cruelty to have attacked them. I did, by way of experiment, gallop after an isolated blessbok (in ordinary times the fleetest of antelopes), and within the distance of half a mile ran him completely to a standstill. A knowing settler made money by stripping off the hides as they lay, and sending them in bales to Cape Town for sale. The poor brutes in their dying agonies always made their way, if possible, to water, and we found their bodies lying in positive heaps along the banks of the small water-courses which we passed on our way to Plaatberg, shortly after the occurrence of this calamity, zebras, blessboks, springboks, and every variety being mixed up together in picturesque confusion.

CHAPTER 19

A Lion Hunt

The officers of the 45th Foot, of whose mess I was an honorary member, had often excited my imagination by their description of the lion hunts which they had enjoyed in the interior. As these expeditions were formidable affairs, extending some hundreds of miles up the country, and entailing the hiring of an ox wagon with its span of twelve or fourteen oxen, I had given up all hope of enjoying that most exciting of sports. Talking one day to an old English settler of the name of Baine, whose farm at Riet Vley, some twelve miles distant, was the favourite resort of the officers of the garrison, he, to my delight, informed me that there was nothing to prevent the gratification of my wish, as there were plenty of lions on his farm, although he could never succeed in convincing the 45th officers of the fact. The latter indeed persisted in making long expeditions in search of what they might find without trouble within easy distance. To convince me of this, he assured me that if I would ride out to his farm early on the following day, without saying anything to my companions, he would undertake to show me lions, and, what was more satisfactory, put me in the way of getting a shot at one.

You may be sure that I lost no time in getting up the next day, and fully equipping myself. I made such despatch that I was with

143

my friend Baine by breakfast time. The same afternoon, having made our preparations, which consisted in *inspanning* his ox wagon which carried our tent, bedding, etc., and saddling our horses, and giving orders to his two bushmen servants, Cobus and Hendrick, to follow, we set out for our encampment, which was situated only ten miles distant, in a pretty mimosa covered valley, bounded by low rocky hills. We had hardly pitched our tent and tethered the horses, when night closed in, and we had the satisfaction of placing the fact of the existence of lions at Riet Vley beyond a doubt, as we soon heard them in their caves on the hills all round us, roaring in the most unearthly manner. So near did they seem, that we heaped our fire with fuel, fearing for the safety of the horses.

We were up next morning at sunrise on the lookout, our object being to try and cut off some stray lion on his way home from the plains; their habit being to prowl about in the night-time in search of their prey, retreating at daybreak, and dragging with them any unhappy beast that might have fallen into their clutches, to feast upon at leisure. We soon found *spoor* which appeared quite fresh, and which, from the spreading out of the feet and toes, left enormous impressions upon the sandy soil. The sun rose high in the heavens, however, and it was well on into the afternoon before we had the pleasure of sighting the animals themselves.

Baine now dismounted his bushmen, and sent them to the summit of the hills, from which they rolled clown fragments of rock, with the intention of driving the lions from their lairs into the open. I had followed the bushmen, leading my horse with the bridle over my left arm and my rifle on the right; and was climbing painfully up the stony sides of the hill, when from behind a mass of rock a few feet on my left issued a tremendous roar—from its proximity rather startling. As I could see nothing of the beast, I descended the hill a little, so as to gain a view of the opposite side of the rock, where I was just in time to catch sight of the brute stealing off, but had no opportunity to get a shot at him. We saw that day at different times some seven or eight fine lions; but so wary were they, and so difficult to distinguish from the soil on account of their colour, that they always escaped us.

I was astonished at the wonderful acuteness of sight displayed by the bushmen, Cobus and Hendrick, who, long before we discovered any sign of lions on the hills, had over and over again detected them, and vainly endeavoured to point them out to us. "See! See! Dar loop de lieuw!" "See! there goes the lion!" they said, as we strained our eyes in the direction indicated, always without result. Their small piercing eyes are wondrously adapted by nature to the purposes for which they are intended, being deeply sunken in their orbits, and shaded from the glare beneath their overhanging brows; supplying them with an almost telescopic power of vision, which is indeed necessary to them as denizens of the boundless flats, for it enables them to detect the game—upon which they are so dependent—at incredible distances, and to follow the slightest traces of a foot-mark, however indistinct—to the extent even of calculating with the greatest certainty the period of time that has elapsed since the impression was made upon the dry *veldt*.

This beautiful adaptation of means to the end proposed, as observable in nature, is nowhere more conspicuous or seen to greater advantage, than in the various forms and peculiarities noticeable in the different species of *ferae naturae* so lavishly distributed over these favoured regions. Take, for example, the ear of the antelope, with its extent of surface and its cup-like form, for the better conveyance of sound; its backward position and direction enabling the timid animal to detect the danger which threatens it from behind; whilst its keen sight warns it of interruption in a forward direction. Take the formation of the hoof of the klip springer, a little antelope only found in rocky districts; which we find provided with a most perfect atmospheric apparatus in the hoof, which being pressed upon the smooth rocky surface, and being provided with a series of minute spongy cells, creates a temporary vacuum, and enables the antelope to maintain its footing. Regard, further, how nature adapts the colour of animals to their surroundings: the tint of the lion's hide to the sandy ground; the plumage of the bird to the bush; and perhaps carried to its greatest perfection in the chameleon, which continually changes its hue, so as to harmonise completely with each different surface with which it comes in contact. Even the inoffensive zebra, which, from its conformation and harmless equine character, would appear at first sight to be defenceless, as seen in the mirage when in rapid motion, becomes quite indistinct from the radiated nature of its robe, and so escapes observation. Well may the psalmist exclaim, *"All thy works praise Thee, O Lord!"*

We at last succeeded in driving a fine male lion off the hills. When he leaped on to the plain, and sighted us, he immediately crouched like a huge cat, facing us and intently watching our movements. It so happened that all our guns, with the exception of my left barrel, had been discharged. Firing a hurried shot, my bullet fell short, just in front of him. Making a pounce at the spot where it struck, he came on into the midst of us with a succession of bounds.

Hendrick was riding an unmanageable brute of a horse, which was so frightened at the lion's sudden advent, that it begun to plunge furiously, and actually succeeded in bucking him off just in front of the advancing brute. We shouted to him to run in amongst our horses, which he did; and never did I see anyone run so fast as the unfortunate bushman—shouting for fear, but holding on to his gun like grim death. Most fortunately the lion took after the horse, which, emulating its master's activity, was soon out of reach. Finding the pace too good for him, the lion crouched again, and coming to a halt we quickly reloaded.

"Now," said Baine, "you wished to kill a lion, here's your chance, go in and win!"

I advanced within thirty yards of the lion, there being no shelter of any kind; but as often as I tried to open his flank, so as to get a shot behind his shoulder (I knew it was of little use firing at his head), so often he turned, always facing me; so, giving it up, I fired at him full front. The ball again fell short; but the second barrel struck him in the foot. His rage was now something awful to look at; every hair of his shaggy mane stood on end. Lashing his sides with his tail, and making a sort of bubbling growl, he came bounding after me.

I was riding a capital shooting horse, which was so accustomed to the chase, that it seemed incapable of fear; and my great difficulty was, that every time I laid the reins over my bridle-arm, for the purpose of raising it to take aim, he would persist in putting his head down to crop the grass and my only chance of getting a quiet shot was to tie a lock of his mane round the bridle, and allow him to do so, with the chance of its falling over his head; in which case I should have stood little chance of escape, the ground being very impracticable from the numerous ant-heaps which made the riding rather dangerous. (I must premise that I was an indifferent shot with ball, and to increase my difficulties was carrying a miserable colonial gun, with one barrel smooth-bored and the other rifled; the great defect of which was that there was no possibility of correcting my second shot by the first, as they had different ranges; and it drove the balls so feebly that I afterwards extracted several bullets which had so little impetus, that they were only slightly grooved instead of being flattened against the bones which they had encountered in their course.)

I fired several shots at the lion in this manner without hitting any vital part; and he made charge after charge at me at full speed, and was sometimes very nearly catching me. I gave him at last a raking shot in the chest, on receipt of which, to my great delight, he went down suddenly on his side. Thinking that it was all over, I dismounted, and, giving my horse to one of the bushmen to hold, walked up to him.

I was unpleasantly astonished, however, when within two or three yards of him, to see him get upon his legs again. I fired a snapshot as he rose, but the ball had only grazed his back, and I was beginning to feel decidedly unhappy, when he staggered and tumbled over, this time for good.

He was a fine black-maned lion, and measured ten feet eleven inches from snout to tail. My companions now rode up. The bushmen speedily skinned him, and pegged out the hide upon the ground, rubbing in wood-ashes from our bivouac fire. On stripping off the hide, we found a quantity of snowy-white fat about his body; but, strange to say, not a trace of *any* kind of food in his stomach. The fat was carefully collected, and I was told, when melted down it made the purest oil for guns, etc., that possibly could be procured. The bladder was seized upon as a great prize by Hendrick, to be converted into a tobacco-pouch, for which purpose it is well adapted from its quality of retaining its moisture; and the skin, with the head attached, was then rolled up and fastened, by way of punishment (as it was very heavy), upon Hendrick's horse; Hendrick, on his way home, heaping all kinds of abuse upon the animal, and occasionally stopping to deliver a vicious kick at the brute, hissing out between his teeth as he did so, in his Dutch *patois*, "Ah, you *verdomde* beast! You'll pitch me off in front of the lion, will you? Take that!" As he basted him at the same time with his formidable rhinoceros-hide *sjambok* (whip) the unfortunate beast had a sorry time of it.

CHAPTER 20

A Farm in the Desert

Baine kept open house at Riet Vley and, as he was a clever, well-educated man and an excellent boon companion, we often paid him a visit. On the flat surrounding his low wattle and daub mansion, roamed herds of antelopes; and one of our great amusements was to set his scratch pack, consisting of some twenty or thirty curs of all varieties of no breed, upon the track of the first herd of wildebeests that approached sufficiently near to afford a chance of overtaking them. When the pack succeeded in coming up with them, they always singled out some particular animal from the herd, and generally contrived in the most cunning manner to hang upon its flanks, and to direct its course right across the farmyard, which they well knew was intersected by a deep trench, made to lead the water off from a pond which stood near, and into this cutting the poor beast would tumble and be soon disposed of. Sometimes they would run their quarry into the pond itself, where they would do their best, by keeping its head under water, to give little chance of escape; Baine or one of his servants generally being at hand ready to give him the *coup de grace* behind the shoulder with his long hunting knife. His flesh, which resembles inferior beef, being too coarse to be palatable, was usually cut up to feed the pack, which might perhaps account for the interest they evinced in the pursuit.

Standing just outside the house was a solidly built mud hut, or shed, fenced in front with stout wooden bars at short intervals. Here were caged two fine lionesses, captured, when cubs, by our host on one of his hunting expeditions, and which had now grown into magnificent animals. The dogs were also the means of supplying these captives with flesh. But meat sometimes ran short, in the absence of the usual herds from drought or other causes, and in this case their meals were speculative. On one occasion, being called away from the farm on business, Baine was detained for nearly three weeks, and on his return found that the game had been so scarce that the lions had not been fed during the whole of that period. Strange to say, however, they were outwardly not one whit worse for their enforced abstinence, being apparently in good health and spirits.

My jolly friend Baine was quite a character, and enjoyed a joke, especially a practical one, beyond everything. The Boers often passed his farm, and would *outspan* their oxen in front of his house without leave, expecting to be entertained. Baine had a great dislike to them, and he used to tell a funny story of the way in which he once got rid of his unwelcome guests. Seeing them on the point of entering his house, having already *outspanned* and turned their oxen loose on the farm, he hastily gave the office to several of his military friends who had ridden out to see him and were satisfactorily employed in emptying certain bottles of strong liquors which were set out for their delectation. By the time the Boers had entered, every one of the initiated had seized on poker, tongs, shovel, and every imaginable instrument capable of sound. The astonished Boers were greeted on their appearance with a concert of the most diabolical description; so that, in vain attempting to get a hearing amidst the fearful din, they were fain, much to their disgust, to return ignominiously to their wagons, under the impression that they had encountered a company of madmen; their exodus being greeted with a shout of laughter on the part of the musicians.

One of the greatest scourges of the sandy *veldt*, and at the same time, without exception, the most cowardly of all the *ferae naturae* with which they are infested, are the hyenas, both spotted and striped. If they can manage to creep up under cover of the night unseen behind any unfortunate animal, they spring upon him unawares. One frequently meets with horses which have been running loose in the plains; and almost invariably, where they have been tied up at night within range of the haunts of these beasts, they are terribly scarred and covered with *cicatrices* from the lacerations made by their powerful teeth, which are almost as formidable as a lion's. They would indeed, from the enormous strength of their jaws, be most dangerous antagonists to man, were it not that their craven nature forbids them to attack any prey that is not to a certain extent powerless to resist them. I once heard, indeed, of a drunken Hottentot, who lying insensible in the *veldt* was dragged some distance by them before assistance came to hand; but have never known any instance of their attacking a man who was on his guard.

A friend of mine wounded a large hyena one day when hunting on the plains; and, having disabled the brute, dismounted from his horse, taking the precaution to load carefully before doing so, and was advancing guardedly towards him. On closer acquaintance, the hyena looked very savage and dangerous; but to his surprise a little Hottentot boy who came from a hut close by, picking up a large stone, ran up to the huge brute and, coolly attacking him with this simple weapon, actually killed him without the least resistance beyond an angry snarl from the cowardly beast. They will not turn even when pursued by dogs or make any attempt to defend themselves beyond snarling and snapping at them in their retreat. When disturbed in their fastnesses in the rocky hills, they start off at a long swinging canter; and, although to all appearance going at no pace, are very difficult to overtake even on a good horse, especially as they keep to the broken ground, and will not trust themselves on the plains if they can avoid it.

Besides the spotted and striped, there is the strand or *stront* wolf (the *aard* or earth wolf of the colonists), another kind of hyena, whose fur is of a reddish tint, and the hunting hyena (about the size of an ordinary dog) a loathsome, unsightly, particoloured brute of sinister aspect, whose mangy hide is bare in

patches. These voracious animals hunting in packs like wolves, run down the most powerful antelopes, taking up the chase in relays when tired so as to have a fresh pack to continue the pursuit; and in this way generally succeed in tiring out their exhausted prey. They are always found in numbers round the remains of any slaughtered beast, which they share with the asvogels and white-crows, which come in crowds to the feast.

The asvogel's power of sight is something marvellous. No sooner is an antelope or any kind of game shot on the plains than these voracious creatures may be seen coming from all directions of the compass, appearing as mere specks in the clear sky, but converging unerringly to the point of attraction. That this is the effect of sight and not scent, as some erroneously suppose, can I think be conclusively demonstrated by the fact, often demonstrated to my own knowledge, that when the slaughtered game is at once covered over with bushes so as to be imperceptible to the sight, they never make their appearance, and it remains unmolested; and this method is invariably practised when the hunter wishes to preserve the game which he may be unable to remove at the time.[1] These hideous birds will, when they get the chance, gorge themselves to such an extent that they are frequently unable to fly, and are easily destroyed; indeed, when suddenly disturbed from their foul banquet, they cannot manage to get on the wing without many previous ineffectual efforts, and are sometimes obliged to partially disgorge the huge quantity of flesh they have devoured, and lighten the cargo, before they can start. They are huge birds, measuring commonly nine feet from wing to wing, and with their fleshy necks denuded of feathers and general loathsome aspect, are altogether the most hideous of the feathered tribe.

Among the most interesting is the secretary bird, which

1. I notice a strong confirmation of my theory of sight *versus* scent in Mr. Boyle's work on the Ashanti war. He notices the singular fact that of the many dead bodies of Ashantis found in the woods, slain by our troops, none of them appeared to be attacked by vultures. Vultures are, of course, common to the whole continent of Africa. The explanation undoubtedly is, that the foliage, from the thick planting of the tropical trees, forms a vast canopy impervious to the outer air. The vulture's vision is thus limited, and his prey unmolested. This appears to me the reasonable solution of the enigma.

may be often met with stalking over the plains in pursuit of his prey, the snake; and so highly are the services of this curious bird estimated by the colonists that they have passed a law exacting a heavy penalty (I believe 100 *dollars*) from anyone destroying it. The manner in which it kills its enemy is very singular. When it discovers the snake, it advances in the most heroic manner to the attack, with its powerful wings outstretched and scarcely giving its enemy time to rear its head in defence, strikes it violently with its pinions once or twice, at the same time stamping upon it with its feet. Then, seizing it with its powerful beak, the bird soars up into the sky, bearing its prey triumphantly to a vast height; when, suddenly releasing it, the reptile falls-prone to the ground below. Almost as soon as it reaches the earth, the secretary bird has alighted, and again advances to the attack, bearing its victim off once more and sending it crashing to the ground in repeated flights until it is quite disabled. This result achieved, the bird commences swallowing its-prey; some of these snakes being of a considerable size, this difficult feat is accomplished in much the same manner as that employed by the snake itself; the membranes of the bird's throat possessing the same expansive power, and its prey disappearing slowly by a series of violent muscular efforts; the protuberance occasioned by its gradually disappearing bulk being plainly perceptible in its passage down the gullet.

The snakes of South Africa are very numerous, and include many varieties. Among the most brilliantly coloured, the *baum slang* (the tree snake) may be enumerated, some of which are resplendent with bright tints of green and gold. They are not very large, seldom exceeding four feet in length. These reptiles ascend trees in pursuit of the young birds. The golden oriole and some other species protect themselves by building their long prehensile nests, which are made of dry grass, at the very extremities of the boughs of some tree, whose outspread branches project over a stream or pool. These nests are very artfully constructed, the entrance being considerably elongated, and only approachable from the detached end, which sways about in the air with every movement of the branch. The Baum slang creeps up the tree, and glides cautiously along the branches, only to find them too slender to bear his weight, and unable to keep his hold, falls into the pool beneath, amidst the excited flutterings, and no doubt hearty congratulations, of the orioles.

"With the exception of the puff adder, which will scarce move out of one's way, I have invariably found every species of snake glad to escape out of sight if possible. This is evidently the instinctive feeling of all the *fercae naturae* with regard to man. I always made a point of pursuing and killing snakes whenever they came across my path, and have had many a chase after them in the long grass as they made away, with their flat heads erect and forked tongues vibrating, often at such a pace that it was difficult to overtake them. No creature is more easy to kill than the snake; a single blow with a stick or a riding-whip being generally sufficient to break the vertebra and disable them. Upon animals, I believe, they exercise a species of fascination, which paralyzes their movements, and prevents their victims from making their escape. The danger is in coming upon them unexpectedly, in which case, when injured, they will naturally rear their heads and strike at you in self-defence. But so far as my experience goes, even the larger *carnivora* will avoid the hunter, and slink away, if possible to do so, without detection.

Before our departure from Bloem Fontaine Sir George Clerk had occasion to go to Plaatberg to arrange matters with the neighbouring tribes, and we paid a visit for that purpose to the Basuto chief, Moshesh, with whom it was important to keep on friendly terms in the interest of the English settlers, who had decided to remain behind rather than give up their possessions in the Bloem Fontaine district. A ten days' march brought us to Plaatberg, where we encamped. We were accompanied by an escort of the 45th Infantry, in addition to the mounted men under my command.

CHAPTER 21

Plaatberg

Plaatberg had been the seat of a Griqua colony, the ruins of whose houses and gardens were still to be seen on the plains below our encampment, having evidently been burnt by the Basutos. The Basuto Kaffirs, under their chief Moshesh, are a numerous and formidable tribe, rich in horses, and so far are unlike the frontier Kaffirs, who, with the exception of the chiefs and a few scouts employed in war time, scarcely ever get on a horse. The Basutos, on the contrary, are seldom seen on foot, and are even at times uncommonly well mounted.

We had not been long encamped at Plaatberg, before the arrival of a mounted Kaffir apprised us of the approach of the chief Moshesh; and we soon after beheld a cloud of mounted Basutos making their way towards our encampment at full gallop. They rode in a confused mass, and, this being a peaceful occasion, were unarmed. They sat their horses in the loosest manner possible, swinging their arms, flourishing their *knob kerries* in the air, and drumming with their naked heels against the sides of their rough steeds; and I was not surprised when they halted and stripped off their rough pads of sheep-skin, which served them for saddles, and were secured to the horse's back by strips of hide, to find a terrible extent of abraded surface underneath. I have never seen backs so fearfully sore as these wretched animals presented; they were positively raw, and made one wince to look at.

In the midst of the throng rode Moshesh, a fine-looking Kaffir, very dark of hue, with a benevolent face; his grey hair giving him quite a patriarchal appearance. He stood over six feet high, and was clad in a plain blue undress staff coat, with infantry trousers strapped over his naked feet, and wore on his head a peaked cap with a gold band. He was perfectly self possessed and well-bred in his manners, shaking hands with Sir George Clerk, and making himself quite at home. He remained for some time, and by means of an interpreter talked over matters with the commissioner, in his marquee, attended by his councillors, two truculent looking savages, who, with the exception of their blankets, were quite naked; and retired, after partaking of some refreshment, accompanied by his followers, with many expressions of good will. The interview was, I believe, very satisfactory, and he expressed his anxiety to be on friendly terms with the Bloem Fontaine colonists, which was the great point to be gained.

It was here that General Cathcart met with so severe a repulse on a former expedition, made at the instance of the colonists for the purpose of demanding compensation for the numerous depredations which Moshesh's followers had committed on their properties and herds. To accomplish this purpose, he made his appearance in Moshesh's country at the head of an armed force, consisting of a division of infantry, and a mounted force of some two hundred Cape-Mounted Riflemen under Captain Somerset, supplemented by a detachment of the 12th Lancers, at that time stationed in the country.

His demands for compensation not having been complied with, this small force made its way into the heart of the Thaba Bossicu mountain, which the chief had made his stronghold, and up the steep sides of which the force had to clamber by the roughest of cattle paths. The infantry had orders to make their advance in another direction, for the purpose of taking the enemy on the flank, and here diverged with that intent. The mounted men had, with much difficulty, achieved the ascent, and were advancing over the tableland, where they suddenly became aware of a swarm of mounted Basutos, who were coming down upon them by thousands, in a tumultuous mass, armed with guns, *assegais*, and short battle axes. On they came yelling their war cry.

It was a moment of imminent peril. The little force could not hope to make any head against such overwhelming numbers. They formed up, however, under the command of Colonel Somerset, and charged repeatedly into the thick of the host. The front ranks invariably gave way as they advanced, but soon closed up again, urged on by the irresistible mass in the rear. At last, wearied and hopeless, the only alternative was to retreat. This they effected in excellent order until they reached the brink of the mountain, which was here unprovided with a path, and very precipitous; their progress being further obstructed by a boundary wall of loose stones, which had been erected to keep the cattle from straying.

This obstacle the Cape Mounted Riflemen easily surmounted. Colonel Somerset's horse taking it at the fly in true hunting style. Several of the men of the 12th Lancers, however, most unfortunately dismounted for the purpose of giving their horses a lead over, and the consequence was, that they were overtaken by the Basutos and killed. Captain Bramley of the Cape Mounted Rifles distinguished himself on this occasion, as indeed he always did, by his cool bravery; remaining behind on the brink of the precipice, and reining in his impatient horse until the actual approach of the foremost rank of the Basutos, when he fired off his pistols in their faces and followed his companions. The infantry, who had reached their ground on the flank of the hill, were also in difficulties, being opposed by a hopelessly superior force, but they accomplished their retreat with little loss, giving a good account of their enemies.

Thus ended the expedition against Moshesh. Terms were subsequently patched up, after a good deal of negotiation with the Basutos, who, happily for us, did not follow up their success, and seemed to rest contented with the advantages that they had gained; but the colonists were sadly disappointed with the unsatisfactory nature of the proceedings, fearing, not without reason, that their prospects, instead of being improved, were now in a still more doubtful position than before. And the General on his return through the Transvaal, encountered, I am told, anything but an enthusiastic reception. He was no doubt hampered by official red-tapeism and Exeter Hall interference, which, as the colonists well know to their cost, have been the fruitful cause of former wars; by repressing anything like energetic measures against our barbarous foe; and on the other side, of positively strengthening their hands against the long-suffering colonist, besides supplying the latter with additional arguments in favour of a separation from the imperial government. The latter indeed, from its isolation and the impossibility of procuring adequate information, was not in a position to adjudicate upon the merits of the various much-vexed questions, so often arising between the natives and the English population.

CHAPTER 22

The Wild Bushmen

The country around Plaatberg is remarkable for the basaltic character of its hills, which form a series of cliff-like projections, overlooking the wide alluvial flats beneath. They are invariably hollowed out on their upper surfaces, as if exposed to the action of water, and impart a very grotesque appearance to the landscape. In the hollows formed by these water-worn excavations exist large caves, which had been made use of as abodes from time immemorial, by the wild Bushmen, who are still to be found living scattered about the plains, and yet retain the evidences of their presence in the blackened surfaces and extraordinary mural decorations of which the wild animals of the *veldt* form the invariable subject. Most spirited and life-like are the rough drawings of camel-leopards, lions, and antelopes, with which they abound; the designs are traced with coloured clays and earthy pigments, that seem to defy the efforts of time to eradicate.

The Bushmen of South Africa present about the lowest type of humanity existing. They are chiefly found in the plains, where they pass a nomadic existence, living in the most primitive of tents, being in fact nothing more than simple lean-to's, made of antelope skins, sewn roughly together with animal fibres (mimosa thorns serving as needles), and are stretched out on sticks upon the windward side, whilst a handful or two of dried grass and leaves, with a skin spread over the interior, serves for bedding, and the ground around is strewed with offal and filth of all descriptions.

I first made their acquaintance when I was riding alone in the *veldt*, and had observed in the distance two Kaffir children, as I thought, roaming about in the long grass. This excited my curiosity, as there was, apparently, no habitation near which might account for their presence. On riding up to them, to my astonishment, they proved to be two little wrinkled Bushmen, habited in skins and armed with diminutive bows and arrows. I came upon them unexpectedly, or I think they would have tried to escape, as they seemed very much frightened and made as if to retreat.

Giving them encouraging signs, I managed to get close to them. They did not exceed three feet five or six inches in height, and had the Hottentot type of feature, but, if possible, of a lower caste. Then-little tufted skulls were bare of covering, and they were perfectly naked, with the exception of a short skin cloak, suspended by thongs from their shoulders. Their brows were plastered round with festoons of the entrails of some animal, several folds of which disgusting membranes encircled their necks, evidently, from their greenish tint, in a state of decomposition. Their speech was as inhuman as their appearance, being nothing more than a series of clicks made with the tongue against their palates, interspersed here and there with a harsh sounding guttural; the different inflexions of these clicks making up their language, a word of some sort being occasionally thrown in, at the rate of a dozen clicks to one syllable. It would puzzle even a missionary to make an alphabet out of it.

Hidden by a depression in the prairie was the usual shed, or lean-to, occupied by a bushwoman, who was nursing a little imp of a child; anything more weird and animal-looking than the pair I never could have conceived. She wore round her waist a fringe of hide cut in strips, which was something, but displayed the same aesthetic taste for decoration as her male companions, and was otherwise quite naked. I am told that they are most omnivorous feeders, and will eat snakes and all kinds of reptiles. Locusts form one of their staple articles of food; drying them in the sun, they pound them between stones into a kind of meal, which they make into cakes (which is, I suppose, their substitute for bread).

They are wonderfully adroit in stalking game, and will creep on their bellies great distances, stopping from time to time and remaining perfectly motionless when they think they are observed, carefully keeping to leeward, that the wind may not carry their scent, and in this manner will actually creep up within a few yards of a lion, and have the audacity to let fly one of their tiny arrows (the bone tips of which have been prepared with some powerful snake or vegetable poison) at the monarch of the waste, which the majestic beast, probably taking for the prick of some thorn, utterly disregards, but which will as assuredly end in his destruction when the treacherous fluid has had time to work as the most deadly rifle-bullet ever launched from a grooved barrel.

These cunning little savages have a clever way of stalking ostriches, and actually succeed in getting quite close to them by means of a screen artfully constructed in the form and covered with the real skin and feathers of that bird. This they push before them, imitating at the same time, with the assistance of the head and neck, which are flexible, the movements made by the ostrich whilst feeding in the most admirable manner, until they can make their approach sufficiently near to effect their purpose.

The Bushmen are irreclaimably wild and untameable. They will at times take up their abode on the outskirts of some Boer's farm, in which case they will do service as herdsmen, looking after their flocks in the *veldt* in return for the protection afforded them; but are never to be trusted, as they are most vindictive when offended, and have been known to make a descent upon a farm where they have been subjected to some supposed slight, and revenge themselves by hamstringing a whole herd of cattle in the most wanton manner. This is sometimes done, however, by way of retaliation, as the Boers are a cowardly race, and think very little of shooting the Bushmen down like dogs when they meet them; and when their thefts are becoming formidable, get up *commandos* against them with the assistance of their neighbours. Standing, however, in great awe of the poisoned arrows, they take the precaution to dismount out of range when attacking them, and advance under cover of their skin *carosses*, which they hold up in front of them as a kind of screen against the deadly little weapons, one scratch from which would be fatal.

It was with unmitigated feelings of regret that I heard the news of our approaching departure from Bloem Fontaine. The affairs of the sovereignty were now in a fair way towards their final adjustment, some of the settlers preferring to remain, others sending in their claims for compensation, which, as is usual in such cases, had to be pared down within decent limits, being very exorbitant. The negotiations between the commissioner and the colonists had been very protracted and vexatious, the scheme of abandonment having been strenuously opposed from the first by the settlers. The store-keepers, who had supplied the troops, saw their prospects of gain vanishing, and were the most obstinate. All these conflicting interests were at last reconciled, and the difficulties successively smoothed away and got rid of by the tact and ability of Sir George Clerk, who was admirably fitted for the task he had undertaken, and who indeed had already distinguished himself in India in many important positions, and who, by his unvarying urbanity and kindliness of manner and disposition, had succeeded in winning golden opinions from all with whom he came in contact.

I was recalled to headquarters before the final settlement of affairs, and did not therefore witness the departure of the troops, but was told that they received the ovation which the popularity and high character of the 45th regiment entitled them to expect. The officers were a most agreeable set, and numbered in their ranks some first-rate sportsmen. I am inclined to think that the big game were the only *inhabitants* of the Bloem Fontaine district that were benefited by their departure.

I left for the purpose of rejoining my regiment in due course, having, at his particular request, parted with my favourite shooting horse to Sir George Clerk's eldest son, who was about to continue his travels further into the interior. The animal was a wonderfully clever beast; I have indeed never seen his superior for large game shooting. He went at racing speed when in pursuit of game, and could be pulled up in his stride within the space of a few yards when required, and on throwing the reins over his head, and allowing them to trail on the ground would remain grazing contentedly for any length of time, with the certainty of my finding him within a few yards of the spot on my return. I could shoot off his back, or point the gun between his ears if necessary, and he carried me along at a fine easy swing, which defied fatigue. Such a horse as this is invaluable for flat shooting; I have had horses that would stand fire well enough, but to get one that could be trusted to remain where you left him for any length of time, was the difficulty. I know nothing more aggravating than a tricky brute, who waits quietly until you come up to him, and when you are just about to catch hold of the reins and re-mount, sends both heels flying at your head, and trots off gently, repeating the manoeuvre every time you approach him, leaving you thirty miles from home perhaps with no one to assist you. I have known an irascible sportsman provoked to such an extent, after a fruitless chase of some miles in this way, that, unable to restrain his temper, he has sent a charge of shot after the brute by way of retaliation. My advice is, if you have got a good horse, keep him!

When I think of the many happy days I have spent in South Africa, and of the sport that may be enjoyed even so far up the country as I have penetrated, and of the many delights presented both to the hunter and the naturalist, with the abundance and variety of beautiful antelopes, and all species of *ferae naturae,* I am only astonished that so few, comparatively speaking, of my countrymen, who have the happiness to enjoy the necessary requirements of leisure and means, do not oftener make the interior of South Africa the scene of their exploits.

LEONAUR

ALSO FROM LEONAUR
AVAILABLE IN SOFTCOVER OR HARDCOVER WITH DUST JACKET

ZULU:1879 *by D.C.F. Moodie & the Leonaur Editors*—The Anglo-Zulu War of 1879 from contemporary sources: First Hand Accounts, Interviews, Dispatches, Official Documents & Newspaper Reports.

THE RED DRAGOON *by W.J. Adams*—With the 7th Dragoon Guards in the Cape of Good Hope against the Boers & the Kaffir tribes during the 'war of the axe' 1843-48'.

THE RECOLLECTIONS OF SKINNER OF SKINNER'S HORSE *by James Skinner*—James Skinner and his 'Yellow Boys' Irregular cavalry in the wars of India between the British, Mahratta, Rajput, Mogul, Sikh & Pindarree Forces.

A CAVALRY OFFICER DURING THE SEPOY REVOLT *by A. R. D. Mackenzie*—Experiences with the 3rd Bengal Light Cavalry, the Guides and Sikh Irregular Cavalry from the outbreak to Delhi and Lucknow.

A NORFOLK SOLDIER IN THE FIRST SIKH WAR *by J W Baldwin*—Experiences of a private of H.M. 9th Regiment of Foot in the battles for the Punjab, India 1845-6.

TOMMY ATKINS' WAR STORIES: 14 FIRST HAND ACCOUNTS—Fourteen first hand accounts from the ranks of the British Army during Queen Victoria's Empire.

THE WATERLOO LETTERS *by H. T. Siborne*—Accounts of the Battle by British Officers for its Foremost Historian.

NEY: GENERAL OF CAVALRY VOLUME 1—1769-1799 *by Antoine Bulos*—The Early Career of a Marshal of the First Empire.

NEY: MARSHAL OF FRANCE VOLUME 2—1799-1805 *by Antoine Bulos*—The Early Career of a Marshal of the First Empire.

AIDE-DE-CAMP TO NAPOLEON *by Philippe-Paul de Ségur*—For anyone interested in the Napoleonic Wars this book, written by one who was intimate with the strategies and machinations of the Emperor, will be essential reading.

TWILIGHT OF EMPIRE *by Sir Thomas Ussher & Sir George Cockburn*—Two accounts of Napoleon's Journeys in Exile to Elba and St. Helena: Narrative of Events by Sir Thomas Ussher & Napoleon's Last Voyage: Extract of a diary by Sir George Cockburn.

PRIVATE WHEELER *by William Wheeler*—The letters of a soldier of the 51st Light Infantry during the Peninsular War & at Waterloo.

LEONAUR

ALSO FROM LEONAUR
AVAILABLE IN SOFTCOVER OR HARDCOVER WITH DUST JACKET

BUGEAUD: A PACK WITH A BATON *by Thomas Robert Bugeaud*—The Early Campaigns of a Soldier of Napoleon's Army Who Would Become a Marshal of France.

WATERLOO RECOLLECTIONS *by Frederick Llewellyn*—Rare First Hand Accounts, Letters, Reports and Retellings from the Campaign of 1815.

SERGEANT NICOL *by Daniel Nicol*—The Experiences of a Gordon Highlander During the Napoleonic Wars in Egypt, the Peninsula and France.

THE JENA CAMPAIGN: 1806 *by F. N. Maude*—The Twin Battles of Jena & Auerstadt Between Napoleon's French and the Prussian Army.

PRIVATE O'NEIL *by Charles O'Neil*—The recollections of an Irish Rogue of H. M. 28th Regt.—The Slashers—during the Peninsula & Waterloo campaigns of the Napoleonic war.

ROYAL HIGHLANDER *by James Anton*—A soldier of H.M 42nd (Royal) Highlanders during the Peninsular, South of France & Waterloo Campaigns of the Napoleonic Wars.

CAPTAIN BLAZE *by Elzéar Blaze*—Life in Napoleons Army.

LEJEUNE VOLUME 1 *by Louis-François Lejeune*—The Napoleonic Wars through the Experiences of an Officer on Berthier's Staff.

LEJEUNE VOLUME 2 *by Louis-François Lejeune*—The Napoleonic Wars through the Experiences of an Officer on Berthier's Staff.

CAPTAIN COIGNET *by Jean-Roch Coignet*—A Soldier of Napoleon's Imperial Guard from the Italian Campaign to Russia and Waterloo.

FUSILIER COOPER *by John S. Cooper*—Experiences in the 7th (Royal) Fusiliers During the Peninsular Campaign of the Napoleonic Wars and the American Campaign to New Orleans.

FIGHTING NAPOLEON'S EMPIRE *by Joseph Anderson*—The Campaigns of a British Infantryman in Italy, Egypt, the Peninsular & the West Indies During the Napoleonic Wars.

CHASSEUR BARRES *by Jean-Baptiste Barres*—The experiences of a French Infantryman of the Imperial Guard at Austerlitz, Jena, Eylau, Friedland, in the Peninsular, Lutzen, Bautzen, Zinnwald and Hanau during the Napoleonic Wars.

LEONAUR

ALSO FROM LEONAUR
AVAILABLE IN SOFTCOVER OR HARDCOVER WITH DUST JACKET

THE LIFE OF THE REAL BRIGADIER GERARD VOLUME 1—THE YOUNG HUSSAR 1782-1807 *by Jean-Baptiste De Marbot*—A French Cavalryman Of the Napoleonic Wars at Marengo, Austerlitz, Jena, Eylau & Friedland.

THE LIFE OF THE REAL BRIGADIER GERARD VOLUME 2—IMPERIAL AIDE-DE-CAMP 1807-1811 *by Jean-Baptiste De Marbot*—A French Cavalryman of the Napoleonic Wars at Saragossa, Landshut, Eckmuhl, Ratisbon, Aspern-Essling, Wagram, Busaco & Torres Vedras.

THE LIFE OF THE REAL BRIGADIER GERARD VOLUME 3—COLONEL OF CHASSEURS 1811-1815 *by Jean-Baptiste De Marbot*—A French Cavalryman in the retreat from Moscow, Lutzen, Bautzen, Katzbach, Leipzig, Hanau & Waterloo.

THE INDIAN WAR OF 1864 *by Eugene Ware*—The Experiences of a Young Officer of the 7th Iowa Cavalry on the Western Frontier During the Civil War.

THE MARCH OF DESTINY *by Charles E. Young & V. Devinny*—Dangers of the Trail in 1865 by Charles E. Young & The Story of a Pioneer by V. Devinny, two Accounts of Early Emigrants to Colorado.

CROSSING THE PLAINS *by William Audley Maxwell*—A First Hand Narrative of the Early Pioneer Trail to California in 1857.

CHIEF OF SCOUTS *by William F. Drannan*—A Pilot to Emigrant and Government Trains, Across the Plains of the Western Frontier.

THIRTY-ONE YEARS ON THE PLAINS AND IN THE MOUNTAINS *by William F. Drannan*—William Drannan was born to be a pioneer, hunter, trapper and wagon train guide during the momentous days of the Great American West.

THE INDIAN WARS VOLUNTEER *by William Thompson*—Recollections of the Conflict Against the Snakes, Shoshone, Bannocks, Modocs and Other Native Tribes of the American North West.

THE 4TH TENNESSEE CAVALRY *by George B. Guild*—The Services of Smith's Regiment of Confederate Cavalry by One of its Officers.

COLONEL WORTHINGTON'S SHILOH *by T. Worthington*—The Tennessee Campaign, 1862, by an Officer of the Ohio Volunteers.

FOUR YEARS IN THE SADDLE *by W. L. Curry*—The History of the First Regiment Ohio Volunteer Cavalry in the American Civil War.